FIELD HOCKEY TECHNIQUES & TACTICS

CLAIRE MITCHELL-TAVERNER

Human Kinetics

Library of Congress Cataloging-in-Publication Data

Mitchell-Taverner, Claire.
   Field hockey techniques & tactics / Claire Mitchell-Taverner. 1970-
     p. cm.
   Includes index.
   ISBN 0-7360-5437-5 (soft cover)
   1. Field hockey. I. Title.
   GV1017.H7M58   2005
   796.355--dc22

                           2004007572

ISBN: 0-7360-5437-5

Acquisitions Editor: Ed McNeely; **Managing Editor:** Wendy McLaughlin; **Assistant Editor:** Kim Thoren; **Copyeditor:** Jan Feeney; **Proofreader:** Bethany J. Bentley; **Indexer:** Betty Frizzéll; **Graphic Designer:** Nancy Rasmus; **Graphic Artist:** Sandra Meier; **Photo Manager:** Dan Wendt; **Cover Designer:** Keith Blomberg; **Photographer (cover):** © Empics; **Photographer (interior):** Craig Wood, unless otherwise noted; **Art Manager:** Kareema McLendon; **Illustrator:** Argosy, Kareema McLendon; **Printer:** United Graphics

Human Kinetics books are available at special discounts for bulk purchase. Special editions or book excerpts can also be created to specification. For details, contact the Special Sales Manager at Human Kinetics.

Printed in the United States of America   10 9 8 7 6 5 4 3 2 1

Human Kinetics
Web site: www.HumanKinetics.com

United States: Human Kinetics
P.O. Box 5076
Champaign, IL 61825-5076
800-747-4457
e-mail: humank@hkusa.com

Canada: Human Kinetics
475 Devonshire Road Unit 100
Windsor, ON N8Y 2L5
800-465-7301 (in Canada only)
e-mail: orders@hkcanada.com

Europe: Human Kinetics
107 Bradford Road
Stanningley
Leeds LS28 6AT, United Kingdom
+44 (0) 113 255 5665
e-mail: hk@hkeurope.com

Australia: Human Kinetics
57A Price Avenue
Lower Mitcham, South Australia 5062
08 8277 1555
e-mail: liaw@hkaustralia.com

New Zealand: Human Kinetics
Division of Sports Distributors NZ Ltd.
P.O. Box 300 226 Albany
North Shore City
Auckland
0064 9 448 1207
e-mail: blairc@hknewz.com

FIELD HOCKEY TECHNIQUES & TACTICS

■ CONTENTS ■

PART I: Mastering the Basics

PART II: Playing the Game

☐ FOREWORD ☐

Over 400 years ago Shakespeare lamented a world in which inherent merit and worth were often not accepted or given their due:

> And right perfection wrongfully disgraced,
> . . . And simple truth miscalled simplicity.

Today, we sometimes also make the same mistake of rejecting that which has been made more easily understandable, and we ought always encourage the search for perfection.

Field hockey is a complex game. A wider variety of skills is required for field hockey than for most other sports such as football or basketball, where the ball is bigger, the game is slower, and fewer moves are available. Accordingly, those who wish to learn and teach field hockey must master the complexity of the game. The way to come to grips with this complexity is to break down the game into its component parts and to tackle them one by one. This is a simple truth. It is what Claire has done in this book.

Claire Mitchell-Taverner was one of the most thoughtful players in the Australian teams that I coached. In embarking on the task of writing a book that outlines the techniques and tactics of the game, she has not only used her own experience but she has also utilised the expertise of many other coaches and players.

None of us is on top of all the details of the game, and each contributor has something extra to offer. In this book Claire has successfully incorporated the contributions of a veritable 'who's who' list of Australian Olympians and coaches. It is testimony to her diligence and status that so many people willingly contributed to this enterprise.

As Claire's principal coach for nearly a decade, I was pleased to see the resonance of my role as a coach in the chapters of this book. Indeed I sometimes felt, as I suspect all coaches feel, that the players weren't listening. Clearly that was not the case with Claire, as many of the principles that I as a coach hold as central to success are covered effectively in this text.

While every hockey enthusiast—whether as a coach, player or spectator—can learn from this book, what I appreciate most is what I have learnt from one of my former pupils. This book offers me some new insights and perspectives on techniques and tactics as well as a reminder of many aspects that can be easily forgotten.

Of course, it is impossible in a book such as this to cover every aspect of this challenging and complex game. Claire has picked up the major threads of the game and explained and illustrated (with more than 100 photographs) their relevance. Additionally, many examples of drills give instructions as to how to put principles into practice. These drills ought also stimulate the enthusiast to create and develop their own training methods and ideas. The aim of every coach must be to create a fun learning environment in which the athletes are challenged.

The essential skills of any game, its building blocks, are covered in part I, Mastering the Basics. These basics must be mastered if one is to become a competent player. Indeed it has long been my view that the complete mastery of these skills makes champion players so reliable and consistent. The basics are the foundation from which champions launch their own special magic. I believe that without highly efficient basics, no one can be classified as a champion player. Indeed, champion players like those featured in this book make these basics look effortless.

Part II, Playing the Game, delves into the vast complexity of how teams of individuals work together with their coaches to build a strategy for playing as a team. The aim is, of course, to score as many goals as possible while limiting opponents' scoring opportunities. Sadly, many coaches approach the game by planning how to limit their opponents' opportunities, and then they think about scoring, which is the most difficult part. I believe the challenge of making goals ought to be the challenge we set for ourselves as coaches and players. If the information in *Field Hockey Techniques & Tactics* can do that, then our game will be stronger and our joy of playing and competing will be greater.

This is a book that can only broaden the knowledge of all who seek to be good at this game. I encourage you to read it.

Ric Charlesworth, FIH Master Coach
Coach of 1996 and 2000 Olympics women's field hockey gold medal teams
June 2004

☐ **PREFACE** ☐

In my field hockey career I played 180 international games; scored 47 times for the Hockeyroos; and collected an Olympic gold medal, World Cup gold, Commonwealth Games gold and three Champions Trophy gold medals. Those accomplishments and the many greater achievements of my team-mates were the result of years of training, hard work, dedication, determination and the repetitive and often tedious rehearsal of the basic skills of the game, all of which were motivated by the enjoyment and reward of being in a successful team environment. This book gives you an insight into the skills necessary for developing your own game to its potential, no matter how big or small your dream.

By drawing on the advice and expertise of past and present champion players and coaches such as triple Olympic gold medallist Rechelle Hawkes, prolific goal scorers Steve Davies and Nikki Hudson, defenders Katie Allen and Olympic gold medallist Matthew Wells, star goalkeeper Rachel Imison and former champion midfielder Kate Starre, in combination with my own experiences as an international player as well as many other experts, I have developed a comprehensive guide of drills and tips that will help you on the road to becoming the best player that you can be. Everyone from ambitious juniors to more experienced players who want to refine their game will find useful tips in this book. Part I focuses on fine-tuning the essential basic skills and also elimination skills, the specialist position of goalkeeping and the important goal shooting component. I don't mean *basic* in the sense that these skills are easy; rather, they provide the necessary skill base for the continued development of your game. Skills such as trapping, passing, tackling and dribbling are central to the game. These skills provide the foundation from which you develop the supplementary skills described later in part I, such as player elimination and goal shooting, and part II. Without the ability to execute the basic skills consistently and competently, you could limit your potential progress as a player. The top players have excellent basic skills, and they spend a long time refining them—that's why they are the best!

Part II applies the skill theory to game situations and explores the higher-end components of playing competitive hockey as a member of a team. You will learn about communicating as a member of a team, awareness of the significance of team orientation, and various strategies for executing penalty corners, other set plays and physical conditioning.

High-level skill development takes time and significant effort. By following the guidelines in this book, you can work your way to becoming a better, more consistent and valuable team player who enjoys playing the game at your highest possible level.

☐ ACKNOWLEDGMENTS ☐

I would like to thank the many friends, players, coaches and hockey specialists who have contributed so much to this book, and for keeping me sane along the way. When Human Kinetics asked me to undertake this project, I wasn't sure exactly what I would be in for, but from the beginning I certainly thought it necessary to ask certain experts for their advice and perspective about particular areas of the game. Although I have played hockey at a high level and have a broad understanding of the skills, I certainly don't consider myself the best authority on every component of the game. These people have significant expertise and worldwide credibility in hockey too, and I believe their generous efforts add enormously to the usefulness of this book for the benefit of players of all ages and stages. Thanks to Michaelangelo Rucci for recommending me to Human Kinetics as a potential author in the first instance and to the ever-patient editors Wendy McLaughlin and Kim Thoren who bore the brunt of my many questions about how and why. Thanks also to my dear Nonna for strongly encouraging me to commit to the project and then to get on with it when I lacked conviction, just as she always does.

Special thanks to current international players Nikki Hudson, Matthew Wells, Rachel Imison and Katie Allen and former stars of the game—many of whom are now enjoying exciting coaching roles worldwide—Kate Starre, Justine Sowry, Lachlan Dreher, Jenny Morris, Damon Diletti, Rechelle Hawkes and Steve Davies who were sensational in their generous and unquestioning willingness to share detailed descriptions of their special skills.

Thanks also to my friends at the Victorian Institute of Sport: Denise Jennings, Toni Cumpston, John Mowat and Dr Stuart Morgan. Toni and John provided much time, support and detailed accounts for chapters 10 and 11. Denise was particularly helpful and generous, going well beyond the call of duty with her significant contribution to chapter 14. All these people, widely considered among the best experts of their particular areas of the game, contributed so much to the project. Much appreciation also to Craig Wood for his thorough, calm, professional and enthusiastic approach to the photography and to VIS scholarship holders Denise, Rachel, Jason, Stacia, Fiona, and Lauren for their patience and necessary good humour during the photo shoot. Thanks to Adam Wallish and Ross Harper at Hockey Victoria for their help with the photos at the State Netball Hockey Centre in Melbourne and also to Linden Adamson and the staff at Hockey Australia for help in providing action photos.

I would especially like to thank and acknowledge my former team-mates and coaches who helped me along the way by making the game so enjoyable and rewarding, day in and day out, even when the going was tough for all of us. Central to that result was Ric Charlesworth who had a major influence on my hockey career and perhaps most significantly, my life away from sport. I thank him not only for his willingness and effort to write the foreword for this book, but for his faith in me, encouragement, brutal honesty when I needed it most, fairness, for challenging me to think and get things right and also for his continued but unspoken friendship from afar.

I was fortunate to have played hockey in an extraordinarily successful team with and for many of the people listed above and thus I was afforded the opportunity to write this book and help other players begin or continue their own exciting journey in this wonderful sport. Again, many thanks to you all!

☐ DRILL FINDER ☐

▢ **KEY TO DRILLS** ▢

▲ Cones

———→ Pass/direction of ball movement

- - - - → Dribble

√√√→ Lead

⇒ Shot on goal

√√√→ Bunt

•••••••→ Player movement

A,B,C... Players/attackers

✖ Defender

✖ Deflector

CO Coach

● Ball

⌡ Stick

Gloves

• Penalty spot

Vulnerable area

T Target

L Line

Tr Trap

P Passer

PO Push out

AMF Attacking midfielder
AS Attacking sweeper
CF Centre forward
CH Centre half
DX Deep defender
DMF Defending midfielder
FL Flicker
FB Fullback
GK Goalkeeper
HB Halfback
H Hitter
IL Inside left
IR Inside right
LH Left half
LW Left wing
M Midfielder
RH Right half
RW Right wing
S Striker
SW Sweeper
DMF Defending midfielder
DEF Defender
2L Second player left
2R Second player right

PART I

MASTERING THE BASICS

All sports are made up of basic skills that athletes need in order to play the game with competence. Although they are called *basic skills,* it doesn't mean these skills are easy, nor are they only relevant for beginners. The top players have excellent basic skills, and they continually refine them—that's why they are at the top of their game.

Hockey is a team sport, so if you consider the cliché that the value of the team is greater than the sum of its parts, you can see that a flashy individual who can't (or chooses not to) make a good simple pass is less valuable on the field than a team-mate who involves other players—usually by performing the basic skills well and often. Of course the appropriate use of 'flair' as an individual is valuable but less so than proficiency in, and willingness to use, the basic elements of the game. Individual brilliance complements a solid game of basic skills.

The basic skills of the game of hockey include trapping, passing, tackling and moving with the ball (dribbling). From here you can develop skills such as elimination techniques and goal shooting, the components that make the game exciting and entertaining for the spectators. Katie Allen and Rechelle Hawkes describe how to develop consistent trapping skills on both sides of your body, and Matthew Wells discusses the various tackling and defensive skills. Nikki Hudson and Steve Davies consider their experiences as outstanding goal scorers. Justine Sowry, Lachlan Dreher and Damon Diletti describe in detail their 'learnings' as top 'keepers turned coaches.

The most important thing to remember is that if you lack sound, consistent basic skills, the other skills will not often be available to you and your game will suffer as a result. The most striking example of such a skill is the basic trap, or stop.

CHAPTER 1

TRAPPING AND RECEIVING

The skill of trapping the ball is necessary all over the field (in defence, attack, midfield and goal-shooting situations), and clean execution of this skill certainly makes that subsequent move easier and available to you more quickly. By consistently using good trapping skills, you are more likely to get the ball in a controlled situation, and you will allow yourself more time to execute the next pass, dribble or goal shot. In order to get the best results for your game from your trap, you have to be prepared as early as possible and balanced for maximum control.

PREPARATION

A common error that players make at all levels is to think about the next action before receiving the ball, so their attention is divided and their execution suffers as a result. Be aware of options before the ball is close, make a clean trap and *then* concentrate on executing the next action. How often do you see a player virtually celebrating a goal before he has made the trap that will set up the goal shot?

   You can trap the ball on your forestick (flat) or your point stick (reverse); regular practice of these different skills is necessary. To reduce the monotony of repetitive practice, focus on this skill when you are doing other drills—you can always practice your trapping, and you should never take it for granted. Remember, without this skill you won't be optimally involved in the game, nor will you get the opportunity to use your other skills.

KEY NOTE
Trapping consistently is about early preparation, concentration on the task, watching the ball and ensuring you have optimal footwork.

Olympic gold medallist Katie Allen is an excellent trapper of the ball. As a result, she is also one of the best defensive penalty corner 'posties' in the game. We will examine that specialist skill in chapter 13.

Katie outlines the following points, which will assist you in making consistent traps in the field of play:

- Begin your preparation to trap the ball as early as you can.
- Watch the ball closely as it moves onto your stick. This may seem obvious, but if you only focus on the ball (one coach told me to actually watch the dimples on the ball) and are not distracted by other elements of the game, you will rarely mis-trap the ball.
- Have a balanced and strong body position. This requires you to move your feet to get behind the ball and have your body weight moving forward. The balance and strength also enable you to move quickly and fluently onto the next skill.
- Stay on your toes; avoid being flat-footed.
- Have the desire and intention to trap each ball that comes your way or anywhere near you.
- Develop an aggressive and positive mind-set.

Positioning Your Stick

Make the big moves early, *then* fine-tune the position of your stick. Anticipate where the ball will arrive, and put your stick and body as early as possible in the position of greatest strength. This will be the position in which you are balanced to make your next move. As the ball gets closer, the adjustment of the angle and the line of your stick in relation to the ball will require finer movements according to the trajectory of the ball and where, in relation to your body, you want the ball to be controlled.

As a general rule, if you want the ball to drop to the right of your body so that you can move in that direction, you need to angle the stick accordingly so that the face opens to the right. Similarly, if you want the ball to fall to the left, open the face of the stick slightly to the left. Early preparation should minimise the possibility of making errors that come about by making last-minute gross adjustments.

If you can keep your stick in an upright position as much as possible (as opposed to a horizontal position), your line of vision will be optimised at the critical moment as the ball approaches. You will also be in a more mobile position that will ensure a smooth transition to the next move. If your footwork is quick, this should often be possible. It is rare that the stick will be completely vertical, but it is better to have it closer to vertical than horizontal at the time that you attempt to make the trap. In instances in which the ball is delivered wide of you and there is no time to move into perfect position, your stick will need to be in a more horizontal position as you stretch to receive.

As you make an upright trap, angle the stick slightly forward (left hand at the top of the stick is forward—further from the body—of the right hand, which is further down the stick and slightly closer to your body) so that the ball drops to the ground in front of you after the trap and doesn't rebound out of your control. (See figures 1.1 and 1.2.)

Also, remember to adjust your stick so that it is square with the line of the ball. Even though you might angle your stick downwards with the aim of getting the ball to drop directly to the ground, try to keep the surface of your stick as close as possible to 90 degrees with the line of the ball if you want the ball to drop directly in front of you. If your stick is on an angle to the right or the left, the ball will take a deflection (as discussed previously), and your control will be messy. (See figure 1.3.)

Figure 1.1 Stick in the upright position.

Figure 1.2 Stick in the horizontal position.

Figure 1.3 Squaring up to the ball.

Positioning Your Body

Ideally, you want to control the ball in the position of greatest strength for your trap. Begin preparing to make the trap as early as you can. You can do this by anticipating where the ball will arrive and positioning your body accordingly.

If you can trap the ball on your flat stick, you should do so as this technique is simpler to execute than a reverse-stick trap. Footwork is critical here; you may simply need to take a couple of steps to the left or right to make sure that you are in the best position to simplify the trap. If you do this, there will be a smaller margin for error, and it will also leave you in a greater position of strength to make a pass or execute an elimination skill.

Be as balanced as you can be, with your feet apart in a wide base. Also, you can protect the ball from the opposition by placing your body between the approaching ball and the opposing player. Make sure that you are mobile in this instance; otherwise the umpire may consider that you are obstructing your opponent.

You can also use the momentum of the ball as it comes onto your stick to receive it in the best possible position for your next move. For example, allow the ball to travel across your body from left to right so that you can make the trap on your forestick. In most instances it is more complicated (and slower) to make the trap on your left and then move the ball into the carrying or passing position on the right of your body. This can be avoided by allowing the ball to travel across your body in the first instance. This principle can apply in many instances, not only when the ball is moving left to right, depending upon your next planned move.

By trapping the ball out in front of your body and away from your feet, you will have better vision of your surroundings once you have controlled the ball. If the ball is under your feet as you control it, your peripheral vision will be reduced because your attention will be entirely focused towards the ground.

If you control the ball out in front of your body, you will also be better prepared for the next move such as a pass, a goal shot or a dribble. Also, it is less likely that the ball will hit your body if you make a trapping error, and you will thus avoid giving away a free hit to the opposition. Keep low with your knees bent, and get your eyes over the ball and you will be well positioned to make a good trap.

Be Confident

If you think you can make a trap, concentrate on doing just that. Too often players 'throw' the stick at the ball in the hope of making a trap, and they seem surprised if they gain control. If you have this 'hopeful' trapping attitude, it means you are not prepared as well as you could be for the next move. Make the decision to go for the trap, move your feet into the best possible position early, be balanced (with your feet forming as wide a base as is comfortably possible), and keep a firm grip on your stick with a 'softer' lower hand (see the section titled 'Catching').

1   DEFENDING THE LINE

Purpose

Practice making a definite trap when the ball is hit in your direction.

Equipment

Two markers, two or three players.

Procedure

Mark a distance of 2 metres (6 feet), and put a marker at either end of the measurement. Player A stands in the middle of the two markers, and player B stands approximately 10 metres (33 feet) in front. Player B pushes or hits the ball firmly between the markers, and player A needs to make the trap. Vary the distance and intensity of the initial push or hit so that player B ultimately makes the shot from a greater distance trying to get the ball past player A.

Variations

You can apply several variations to this drill.

- Variation 1: Increase the width of the trapping area so that player A needs to move left and right to make the trap. Increase the competitiveness by keeping score between the players who will alternate roles. For example, player B tries to hit or push past player A. (See figure 1.4.)

- Variation 2: Once both players are comfortable with the previous drills, introduce a third player who tries to steal the ball from the player making the trap. Player B tries to hit past player A, who traps, controls the ball and makes a pass to a target (a player or a cone). Player C waits for the trap to be made before trying to jump on the rebound. Player A needs to control the ball from the initial trap in order to prevent player C from stealing the ball.

- Variation 3: You can increase the distance between the markers so that two or three trappers (players A, D and E) are on the line; then use two or three players (F, B and G) to alternate hitting and pushing from different angles in an effort to get the ball across the line and past the trapping players. (See figure 1.4.)

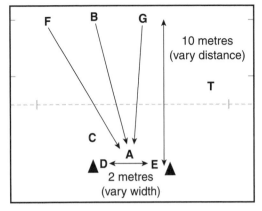

Figure 1.4   Defending the line.

CATCHING

When you catch a tennis ball with your hands, you move your hands with the motion of the ball until it is controlled. With a hockey stick, your right hand may be a little 'softer' than your left hand and 'give' a little to minimise the extent to which the ball bounces off the stick.

Your left hand is always tight at the top of the stick to control the movement of the stick, and your right hand plays more of a guiding role, which means it needs to be softer than your left hand. Move your stick to meet the ball a little earlier or further in front of your body than you would if you were just blocking the ball, and move with the momentum of the ball until it is controlled. (See figure 1.5a-c.)

Figure 1.5   Meet the ball early and give with the momentum of the ball until it is controlled.

(continued)

7

Figure 1.5 *(continued)*

2   TOSS AND CATCH

Purpose

To become familiar with the concept of 'giving with the ball' as you control it on your stick using a 'catching' technique.

Procedure

Tap the ball on the toe of the stick, and then try to catch it rather than tap it into the air again. When you can do this, try tossing it back into the air and catching it again. See how many throws and catches to yourself that you can do without dropping the ball to the ground. You and a partner can also throw the ball back and forth; to measure your improvement, you can count the number of catches you make.

By watching the ball and especially the technique of the player delivering the ball, you can improve the quality of the trap by watching to see how it is being delivered. It may be bouncing, a slow mis-hit, powerful or raised. Then you can prepare for the trap accordingly. Scan your surroundings before the ball gets close, then focus on the ball as it approaches.

3   SCAN, THEN TRAP

Purpose

KEY NOTE
Scan your surroundings, but be careful not to be distracted by your next move, even if you think the trap is an easy one.

To introduce the idea of scanning ahead to be aware of the surroundings before making the trap.

Procedure

The player receiving the ball looks up at a second player downfield, who is holding fingers up. The receiving player shouts out the number of fingers that they see before concentrating on the trap. The signalling player can move around as in a game situation.

The following are key points to focus on when trapping the ball.

- *Positioning your hands and knees.* Your left hand remains at the top of the stick, and your right hand is lower down on the stick, as is usually the case in general play. Hockey players are notorious for having bad backs, so if you remember to bend your knees, your back will thank you in the long term!

- *Bending your knees.* By bending your knees you will also get your eyes closer to the ball, make a more confident and reliable trap and maintain good peripheral vision of your surroundings. As a result, you will be in a position to make the best decision about what to do when you do control the ball. By maintaining a low centre of gravity by bending your knees, you will be strongly balanced when you receive the ball and less vulnerable to the push and shove of an opponent. (See figure 1.6.)

- *Trapping in a stationary position.* Usually, the more time you have, the more likely you'll be to make a good trap. But it is easy to become complacent and make the next pass in your mind before you have the ball, particularly if you think you have plenty of time. This can result in clumsy errors.

Figure 1.6 Bending your knees and making a wide base help to give you balance, strength and physical presence which protect you from physical contacts by your opponents.

It's unusual not to move when you're making a trap, so pay attention to your footwork, even if you think you have all the time in the world. Good footwork requires you to get behind the ball and in the best position to ensure a quick transition to the next play. You'll see lazy footwork in players reaching for balls and making unnecessary half traps because they don't get their eyes and body into the best position. Remember, there is no such thing as an easy trap!

If you're stationary, there is a smaller margin for error, but you should still pay close attention to the detail of trapping. Your footwork will get your body in a balanced position and your eyes in line with the ball.

- *Receiving on the move.* This is more difficult than the stationary trap, so you must pay attention to this skill, too. Preparation is the key, and you must get yourself into your most balanced position as early as possible so that when you make the trap, the next movement is simple. Try to receive the ball while moving forward and towards your attacking goal when you have the time and space to do so. Avoid the temptation to receive the ball as you're facing away from the direction in which you want to move, because it will slow down the transition to the next play.

Whether you are surrounded by goal-hungry forwards, tenacious midfielders, or dogged defenders, you need to minimise the distance that the ball rebounds off your stick when you make the trap. You need to be strong as you receive and trap the ball in the circle. Refer to the previous Defending the Line drill for additional practice.

Sneaky forwards often allow defenders to make the trap in the circle (the hard part), then the forwards pounce on the spillage and steal the possession (the easy part). In other situations which are not so tightly contested, you may be able to receive the ball by bunting it into space so that you can run onto it unchallenged.

4   HOLDING YOUR GROUND AS YOU RECEIVE

Purpose

To practice maintaining your strength as you make the trap in anticipation of a defender's attempt to bump you off the ball.

Procedure

Set up the drill so that each attacker is marked closely by a defender. When the attacker is about to make the trap, the defender (gently) nudges the forward to try to get him or her off balance. The forward needs to concentrate on maintaining balance, keeping a wide base and making the trap with strength.

By trapping the ball as far inside the field as you can, you can maximise the space available to you (and increase your options when you do receive the ball). If you receive the ball very close to the sideline, you limit your movement and passing options in the next play. But if you receive the ball further inside the field, you increase passing and elimination options on both sides of your body and on both sides of your opponents. Sometimes you will have no choice but to receive on the boundary of the field of play, but usually you will. Often players in the wing-half position receive the ball right on the sideline when they have space to receive infield instead. On the sideline, they decrease their passing and moving options.

Claire Mitchell-Taverner in action for the Hockeyroos during their Olympic gold-medal win in 2000.

• *Planning ahead.* Preparation is the key to receiving the ball cleanly and getting a good return for that hard-earned possession. Before you receive the ball, have an idea of what you want to do when you earn possession. Then set your body position early and control the ball.

Make every effort to receive the ball while facing or moving forward, as this makes for quick transition and gives you an opportunity to assess your options and obstacles with good vision once you have the ball. Becoming a proficient receiver also encourages your team-mates to pass to you with confidence when they have several passing options.

Be aware of your options before you get the ball. While you have time and before you make your lead and receive the ball, divide your attention among the ball, the passer and the positions of your team-mates and opposition players off the ball.

When you are trapping you have a lot of information to digest in a short time, so make a habit of assessing your surroundings when you are not directly involved in the play. Do this at training and during matches, and eventually it will become a natural, automatic thing for you to do under pressure.

• Receiving in a position of strength. If you are unable to receive the ball in space and moving towards your goal, you might find yourself in a tight situation in which you need to have your back to your attacking goal. A defender could be marking tightly or making position between you and your attacking goal. This is often the case in tight midfield situations, and this technique of trapping with your back to your attacking goal and your opponent can buy you time to assess your options. (I elaborate on some of these movements in chapter 4.)

One option is to make a short, sharp lead back to the ball and roll in an arc left or right so that you move forward as soon as possible, once you have received the ball. If you are moving when you receive, it is more difficult for your opponent to gain possession with a clean tackle, and the umpires are less likely to call you for obstruction.

5   LEADING IN AN ARC

Purpose

To practice receiving the ball so that you can quickly move forward, even when you need to lead backwards to get the ball.

Procedure

Player A passes the ball to player B, who leads towards the ball to receive. Player B receives the ball and tracks in an arc so that ultimately he or she moves forward (as in figure 1.7). Use a marker or a third player as the defender who is passive to begin with. You can practice this drill by moving in an arc to the left and the right.

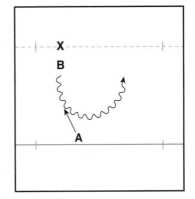

Figure 1.7   Receiving in an arc.

You can use your body to move the defender away from the area in which you want to receive the ball. This doesn't have to be a gross movement; in fact, it can be as simple as a transfer of weight or a short lead. A sharp movement of the stick can also be enough to sell a dummy to your opponent. This dummy will create space for you by getting your opponent off balance and reacting to your move.

• Receiving the ball in the air. Even seasoned players make the mistake of lifting the stick to trap an airborne ball. If you always keep your left hand higher in the air than your right hand as you are trapping a raised ball, you are unlikely to make a foul when executing this skill.

If you don't have time or space to let the ball drop to the ground first, get under the drop of the ball and use a soft right hand if the ball is moving slowly, and keep your stick on the ball as it drops to the ground, ready for the next move. If the ball is moving more quickly and towards you rather than dropping down to you, keep your stick angled towards the ground (as for other trapping techniques) so that the ball drops at your feet.

Slip Trap

This is another method of trapping and receiving the ball. Use this when you receive the ball from behind as you move forward. To do this on your left side, catch the ball from behind and outside your left foot and direct the momentum of the ball onto your right side (your forestick side). The ball is then in a position of strength for you, and you have not stopped moving forward. The opposite is the case when the ball is delivered from behind you and to the right of your body so that you can receive the ball on the move. Slip it across your body to your left side in one movement. (See figure 1.8.)

Figure 1.8 Receive the ball on the left and slip it across your body to your flat-stick side.

6	SLIP TRAP

Purpose

To practice receiving the ball from behind while moving forward and executing the slip trap across your body.

Equipment

Two markers, two players.

Procedure

Player A passes the ball gently to player B, who is moving forward. Player B collects the ball on his or her reverse side and moves it across the body to the forestick side. Increase the intensity of the pass and the speed of the trap as you become more comfortable with this movement. Do this from left to right and from right to left.

Reverse Trap

Three-time Olympic gold medallist Rechelle Hawkes was one of the most reliable reverse-stick trappers I played with in my time with the Hockeyroos. It is no accident that Rechelle, who had excellent basic skills and was an outstanding trapper, was also one of the greatest female players ever. Her game epitomised consistency. The following are her tips for the difficult skill of reverse trapping:

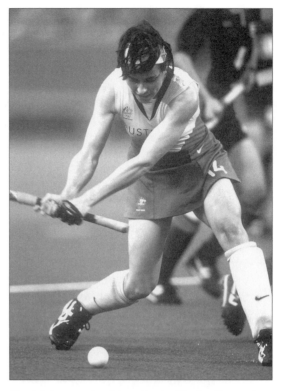

- First, make sure you have your body on the correct line with the ball.
- Line the stick up with the ball early and prepare for the trap with your stick in a comfortable position.
- In most instances, trap slightly in front of the body and in front of your right shoulder, about one stick length in front of your body and on the line of your right foot. Remember that you want to receive the ball in good position to execute the next action.
- Make sure the angle of the stick is square with the ball, as in the case of the forestick trap.
- Be balanced to maximise the transition to the next play, with your weight distributed evenly between your feet. (See figure 1.9.)

'A mistake people often make is allowing themselves to get distracted by things going on around them, so the skill becomes reactionary. You need to plan the trap, not react to the situation at the last minute.'
—Rechelle Hawkes

Figure 1.9 Trap the ball in line with your right shoulder so you have the ball in the position of greatest strength (on your forestick) for the next move.

When receiving the ball on your reverse, get your head and eyes over the ball or close to it. If you have time, have your right leg forward so that your eyes are over the ball when you make the trap. Keep your stick close to the ground, and watch the ball.

On synthetic surfaces many players get lazy and use a low-to-the-ground, flat-stick method to trap on their reverse. This is a safe option, but it is not ideal in tight situations because once you make the trap, you will be slow to get back to an upright position to make the next move. Try to develop your ability and confidence to make an upright trap in all situations, because transition to the next move is easier, your vision will be improved and you will have a greater awareness of the positions of other players.

USING DUMMIES OR FAKES

In some situations you will have time and adequate body position to allow the ball to travel across your body from left to right, so you can control the ball on your forestick after making a dummy to do the opposite.

You can sell a dummy to a defender by transferring your weight as though to receive the ball on your left foot, in so doing committing the defender to that side. Then you can let the ball travel further to the right, across the body of the defender so that the ball ends up on his or her reverse (the defender's weaker side). When you receive the ball, the defender will have his or her weight still moving in reaction to your dummy, which is not good preparation for a player who is trying to win possession. In this situation you will receive the ball out in front of your right foot and in a position of strength, and the defender will need to react to this from a less than ideal position thanks to your successful dummy.

In some instances the best option is to execute the basic dummy from right to left in the same manner, but it is a more difficult skill and requires you to receive the ball on your reverse-stick side, which is a more vulnerable position. The ball is also in a better position for the defender to dispossess you because you are more likely to have the ball on his or her flat-stick side.

So to receive the ball on your left foot and on your reverse-stick side, move as though to receive the ball on your right side and on your right foot, with a reverse-stick trap. When the defender moves to react to this and the ball is almost on your stick, move your stick across the face of the defender with the momentum of the ball, and control it on your left foot with a reverse-stick trap. The defender will probably be watching your body movement, not the ball, as you move to receive, and he or she will need to react to your late change. If you eliminate your opponent with this move, cut in immediately behind the defender to make sure that player doesn't have a further influence in that play. (See figures 1.10*a-c* and 1.11*a-b*.)

Sometimes you can greatly affect the play by not touching the ball at all. If one team-mate (player A) is in the same line of the ball as another team-mate (player B), the first player (player A) can move as though to trap the ball, and in so doing commit the immediate opponent to that end. The opponent (player C), who is likely to be watching the movement of the first player and not the ball, will commit to making the tackle or an interception on the first player (player A). At the last second (when the ball is almost trapped), player A lifts the stick and allows the ball to pass through to the team-mate (player B). The opponent will not have time to react to this and will be overcommitted to the original intended tackle. (See figure 1.12.)

Figure 1.10 (*a*) Basic dummy left to right starting position, (*b*) basic dummy left to right end position. (*c*) Cutting in behind.

Figure 1.11 (*a*) Basic dummy right to left starting position, (*b*) basic dummy right to left end position.

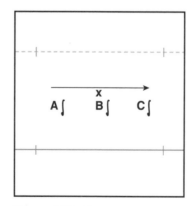

Figure 1.12 Dummy trap.

Many experts of the game consider the trap the most important skill because, without the ability to make a trap and receive the ball in a controlled position, you limit your opportunities to make an impact in a game situation. Without possession of the ball, you can't make a pass, move with the ball or have a shot on goal. Obviously, there are other ways to earn possession, which we discuss in subsequent chapters, but most of your possessions in fluid play will result from trapping and receiving the ball.

Try to keep the trap as simple as possible, which usually means making the trap on your forestick. This is not always possible, so you need to be able to receive on your reverse side also. In both instances you should have some awareness of your surroundings for the moment when you need to execute the subsequent move—be it a pass, dribble or goal shot.

Early preparation is critical. This involves some recognition of the trajectory of the ball and anticipation of its speed and the nature of its travel: Is it travelling flat along the ground? Is it bouncing? What could change between the delivery and your trap? Sharp and early footwork is optimal, as is early preparation of the positioning of your stick according to your next planned move. Value the significance of the trap and develop your ability to execute it in all possible situations, and you will be in excellent position to improve your overall game.

□ CHAPTER 2 □

PASSING

No matter what your position is on the field, you need reliable and flexible passing skills. The various passing techniques allow you to transfer the ball to team-mates, and each provides a varying degree of subtlety and power. You need to develop your ability to execute these passing skills while in both a stationary position and moving at speed.

To be an effective passer means that you will become a better team player in attack, in the midfield and in defence. Quality passes bring your team-mates into the game, keep your opponents guessing about your next move, give you confidence to relieve defensive pressure and create exciting attacking opportunities for your team. Some common passing techniques include the push pass, hit, upright and flat slaps, reverse-stick pass, bunt and deflection, and the overhead pass. The following four drills can be used to sharpen your general passing skills.

7   PASSING AWARENESS

Purpose

To make firm and accurate passes in a defined area while being aware of your surroundings before receiving the ball; communicating effectively with your team-mates and thinking ahead of the play.

Equipment

One to three balls, four to ten cones or witches hats, five to ten players

Procedure

Place cones evenly in an area covering 10-20 metres. For example if there are eight players, place one player on each cone and two players on two or three cones. Beginning with one ball, the first player passes to a player on a different cone and then usually follows their pass. The ball movement continues in this manner. The passes must be made to a player on any cone and the players must try to fill all the cones so that there is never a cone without a player on it. It may be that the players do not always follow their pass but fill spaces on the other cones when appropriate. The drill is quite difficult to get right and requires all the players to be aware of where the other players are positioned. Add a second and then a third ball so that the players must be aware of the position and movement of all the balls before receiving the ball, make quality traps and passes and also move between the cones as though making leads to the appropriate area.

8   RECEIVE AND PASS

Purpose

To practice combining the receiving skill with the distribution skill.

Procedure

Receive the ball from another player and, using one or all of the techniques outlined in this chapter, make the pass to a stationary target or a moving target. Vary the distances over which you pass, and be sure to practice all passing techniques. Make the transition from the trap to the release of the ball as slick and quick as possible while maintaining the quality in your execution. Count the hits on the target in sets of 10.

9   RECEIVE AND PASS WITH VISION

Purpose

To combine the skills of receiving, passing and maintaining good vision in an urgent situation.

Procedure

Set up three stationary targets. Receive the ball as in the first drill, but, as you receive the ball, have a coach or another player call out to you which target you are to hit. You can test your peripheral vision by having players act as the target, and you make the pass to the one that puts his or her hand in the air. Try to minimise the time between making the trap and hitting the target, and use all the passing techniques.

10   BASIC HITTING DRILL

Purpose

To encourage accuracy when hitting on the move while maintaining an awareness of what is happening in other areas of the field. Also provides good trapping practice.

Procedure

Set up the cones as per the full field diagram and place a player on each cone. Players A and F begin with a collection of balls at each end of the field and the balls are passed (one from each end at a time) as per the diagram with the passer following their pass. The final pass ends in a goal shot and the shooting players (players E and J) sprint around the field to begin again by passing the ball from the opposite end. There should be two balls moving in the area at one time but in opposite directions. (See figure 2.1.)

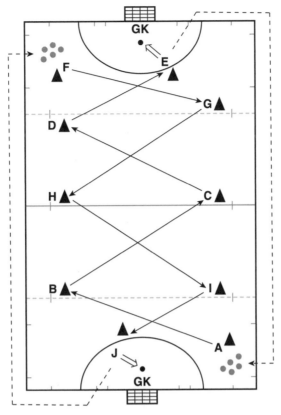

Figure 2.1 Basic hitting drill.

PUSH PASS

This is a passing technique that you can develop into a well-disguised and accurate option for moving the ball over short distances. Accuracy is important, and passing the ball with a push is a particularly accurate passing option.

The push pass is a good choice in tight situations, primarily because your stick doesn't need to leave the ball, which makes it a quick shot to execute. It is also difficult for your opponent to steal the ball from you because your stick remains in contact with the ball until it is released.

Because there is no backswing involved, the push pass is not only one that you can make quickly and in confined space, but it is also a deceptive pass that gives few clues to your opponent about when or in which direction the pass will be made. Quick footwork is necessary for getting your body into the optimal passing position; but if quick footwork is not possible, you still need to be able to execute the skill. The speed required is largely determined by the time available to get the body into the best position to execute the skill with strength and accuracy. In a situation where you have time to prepare, quick footwork will get your feet lined up so that together (left foot in front of right) they are pointing in the anticipated direction of the pass or the target.

The strongest passing position is 'off' your left foot, which means that with your feet lined up to point in the direction of the target, your weight is transferred from your right leg to your left leg, so you are pushing 'off' your left leg. This will give you maximum weight transfer and strength, but power is not always the most important component of the pass.

You can push 'off' your right foot when you are on the move and short of preparation time. If you don't have time to prepare perfectly, you will be unable to get your feet in the ideal position (left foot in front of right and in line with your target) to generate the power that is possible when you have more time. If it is power you are after, pushing off your right foot is not the ideal option. But it can catch your opponent unaware, which in some situations is a more valuable result. You will sacrifice power if you push off your right foot, because your weight will not necessarily move through the ball in the direction that you are trying to pass the ball. Your footwork suffers when you are rushed for time. In this instance it will be more natural for your weight to move across the line of the pass (towards your left foot) than towards your target, which will reduce the power you are able to generate. Power is not always the most important characteristic of a pass! (See figures 2.2 and 2.3.)

Figure 2.2 Push off the left foot.

Figure 2.3 Push off the right foot.

To make the push pass, keep your right hand low on the stick (in a comfortable dribbling position), your knees bent and your stick on the ground. With the ball between your feet, follow through so as to transfer your weight from your back leg to your front leg. For maximum strength and accuracy, try to get your stick and body weight to follow through in the direction of your target.

11 PUSH PASS WITH POWER

Purpose

A drill to help you improve your passing power while maintaining your accuracy.

Procedure

Move with the ball towards your target and release the ball at a predetermined point. Use a speed gun to measure the speed of the ball, and try to make the pass as firm as possible while also hitting the target. If you don't have a speed gun, ask another player or a coach to use a stopwatch to measure the time taken for the ball to leave your stick and hit the target. You can use the goal circle for this drill: Move to the top of the circle, make the pass at that point, and aim at the targets in the bottom corners of the net.

THE HIT

Hitting the ball gives you extra power, so this is a good option when you want to pass the ball firmly over a long distance. You can hit off either foot, although as with the push pass, you will get more power if your left foot is forward of your right foot and your weight is transferred in the direction of your target from your right (back) leg to your left (front) leg.

In rushed situations, such as when you are shooting for goal, it may be best to hit off your right foot to achieve the 'surprise factor' and catch the opposition unaware. But in this situation there is less opportunity for good weight transfer towards your target, and as a result you may lose power.

Here are some simple points to remember:

- Point your shoulder and your feet towards your target.
- Bend your knees so that you have a low centre of gravity.
- Line the ball up so that it is level with your left foot.
- Keep your hands together. Many young players (especially young girls) try to hit with their hands apart, so they find it difficult to get optimal power.
- Focus your attention on the back of the ball.
- Follow through towards your target to transfer your weight in the direction you want the ball to travel.

With careful execution and lots of practice, you can also use the hit as a deceptive pass. Jenny Morris, one of the Hockeyroos' best defenders and a double Olympic gold medallist, was very good at distributing the ball with a hit. She also mastered the technique of hitting the ball off her right foot (the equivalent of an 'off forehand', or a slice in tennis).

These are Jenny's tips for executing this skill:

- Ensure that the ball is positioned in the middle of your stance, as compared to hitting normally where the ball is positioned slightly out in front of the left foot.

'The pass is generally made to the right – that is, looking left and making the pass to the right.'—Jenny Morris

- It is generally easier with a shortened grip rather than with your hands at the top of the stick.

- Peripheral vision is important because you need to know where it is you want to make the pass while glancing to the left and then clipping the ball to the right.

- Remember, all you need is a slight weight transference in the opposing player. Often that is all that is needed to create the gap.

- Make sure your team-mates know that you are capable of making this pass so they expect it, even when you are not looking at them.

- I cannot emphasise enough how this is a hitting action driven from your wrists, with very little upper body and shoulder movement but plenty of leg power (your knees are bent and feet pointing as if you are at least hitting the pass in a straight direction).

- The wrists dictate how much of an angle you are putting into your pass—feet position stays the same, opening of the wrists is the key.

This passing technique looks as though you are hitting through the ball, but the technique in which you open the face of the stick at the point of contact can result in a pass being sliced across the face of a defender from your left to right (the opponent's right to left).

UPRIGHT SLAP AND FLAT SLAP

The slap shot is a faster shot to execute than the hit because it requires a shorter backswing. The slap can catch your opponent unaware, so it is particularly useful in the attacking circle, defensive circles, as well as in other areas of the field too. The two kinds of slap shots are the upright slap and the flat slap.

For the upright slap, your hands are apart (perhaps in the dribbling position), your stick is close to upright and the ball is fairly close to your body. You are effectively hitting the ball, but the backswing is shorter and your hands are apart. You will not generate the same power you can with a hit, but it is a quicker shot to execute. (See figure 2.4.)

For the flat slap, the ball is further away from your body. Bend your knees and slide your stick, which is horizontal, along the ground during the backswing. When you follow through, keep the stick moving along the ground and make contact with the ball just below the head of the stick. Keep your hands together. In the attacking circle, you can angle your stick backwards (the upper edge is behind the lower edge) to raise the ball at goal. (See figure 2.5.)

This slap shot can be used as a deceptive way to pass because you can be looking at one potential target (straight ahead), sell the dummy with your backswing, then hit across the line of the ball to make a more penetrating pass forward instead (see figure 2.6). Also, it is a useful and often unexpected goal shot in the circle.

Figure 2.4   Performing the upright slap.

Figure 2.5   Performing the flat slap.

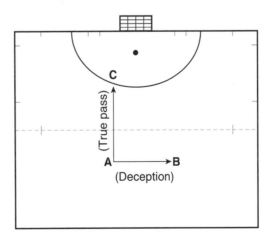

Figure 2.6   The flat slap is a deceptive, power-ful, penetrating passing technique.

REVERSE-STICK PASS

This is a difficult skill to perform with strength and over distance, but it is a useful, short, sharp pass. Have the ball in front of your right foot and your weight on your right foot. Have your head over the ball and make sure your hands are apart for added strength and power. With a short backswing, tap the ball towards your target. The lower down the stick you can place your right hand, the more power you will generate. (See figure 2.7.)

Figure 2.7 The reverse-stick pass is useful over short distances. Make sure your weight is over the ball.

You can hit the ball on your reverse side also, but this is a low-percentage passing option and would most likely be used as a last resort because of its high level of difficulty. Very few players can execute this shot with consistency.

This reverse-stick hitting technique might be useful in the left attacking corner of the field when you don't have time to get your feet around and make a regular cross into the circle. In this instance keep your hands together but lower down the stick than for a forestick hit in the general field of play when you have plenty of time. Try to get your head over the ball, and hit off your right foot with a compact backswing. A compact backswing provides a smaller margin for error, whereas a big 'wind-up' in your backswing can be difficult to control, and you are less likely to make clean contact with the ball.

12   REVERSE-STICK PASS

Purpose

To develop confidence and strength when passing on the reverse side of your body.

Procedure

Use three players in a triangle formation. The players pass the ball around the triangle using the reverse-stick passing technique. Alternatively, you can pass in pairs in the same manner or onto a rebound board if you are on your own.

13 GENERAL PASSING AND DUMMYING

Purpose

To practice moving with the ball and passing by using a reverse-stick (or a flat-stick) pass and a dummy trap as described in chapter 1.

Procedure

In lines of three players, begin with the ball in the middle with the central player. The central player (player B) tracks forward and left, then makes a firm reverse-stick pass to player C. Player A tracks forward into the central position and dummies convincingly over the pass. Player C receives the ball and then tracks left with the ball to make a reverse pass to player A with player B dummying over the ball. Continue alternating in this way so that in the third play, player A tracks left and passes through player C to player B on the far right side of the drill. (See figure 2.8.)

Variation

Practice the dummy going the other way by using flat-stick passes.

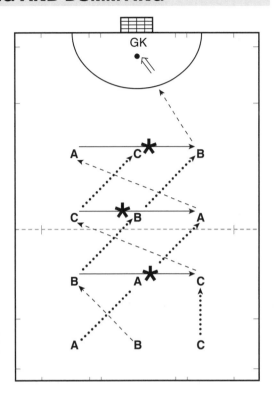

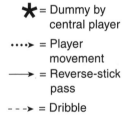

✳ = Dummy by central player

····▶ = Player movement

——▶ = Reverse-stick pass

---▶ = Dribble

Figure 2.8 General passing and dummying drill using the reverse-stick pass over short distances.

BUNT AND DEFLECTION

You might not think of the bunt as a passing option, but it is a useful passing technique over a very short distance for situations where you are tightly marked and don't have time or space to gain control. A bunt is a one-touch technique in which you knock the ball (without trapping it) to a team-mate who is close by or running past you. You can angle your stick according to where you want the ball to travel, in the same way as we discussed angling your stick to trap the ball in chapter 1.

The bunt technique might be useful for you if you are a midfielder who is unable to safely receive the ball in a tightly marked contest. Instead of trying to make a trap that will result in a 50/50 contest with an immediate opponent, you can bunt the ball to the left

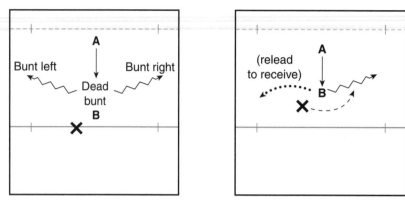

Figure 2.9 Bunting to the left, dead bunt and bunting to the right.

Figure 2.10 Releading.

or right or make a dead bunt (almost trapped) slightly back in the direction from which the ball has travelled for a running team-mate. In the next move, you can quickly relead (taking your immediate opponent away from the area in which you've bunted the ball) and receive the ball in the second play. (See figures 2.9 and 2.10.)

You can bunt the ball to either side of your body according to the position of your immediate opponent and the position of your team-mates. The bigger the backswing of your stick, the further you will bunt the ball as you 'one-time' it in the desired direction, but this will also increase the level of difficulty. The dead bunt requires very little, if any, backswing—it is almost a trap from which the bunter moves away quickly to make another lead.

In the same way that you use a bunt, you can use the deflection in the general field of play (not only in the attacking circle) when you are not in good position to control the ball for your own immediate use. Players' positions change quickly in the dynamic game of hockey, so if you spot an available player upfield, you will need to execute a pass quickly without the luxury of making a trap. A deflection is the perfect solution in this situation.

A deflection changes the line of the ball as it travels with speed. It is a deceptive and subtle passing technique that requires you to angle the stick to determine the angle of the pass and eliminate a tight-marking defender with one deft touch. This might be useful for you if you are a midfielder who can see a space ahead for a striker to run into. A slight touch on the ball will eliminate the deflecting player's immediate opponent, and the striker or receiving player can collect the ball higher up the field.

Be aware that a deflection is often a risky technique if the second player (the striker in this instance) is not aware of the deflector's intentions. A turnover will be the likely result in this instance, so make sure that if you are using this technique you do so in a safe (attacking) area of the field. This will mean that if the ball is turned over to the opposition, the result is not an immediate attack on your deep defenders.

This principle of making wise decisions according to the area of the field that you are working in applies to all higher-risk techniques. There are areas of the field in which you should not risk turning the ball over, and there are safer areas of the field in which you can attempt trickier skills (such as those described previously) because a turnover would not be so damaging. See figure 2.11 for areas of the field considered safe and dangerous.

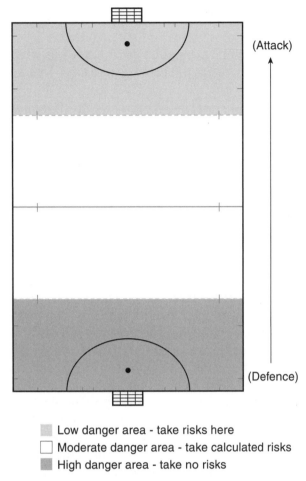

(Attack)

(Defence)

▨ Low danger area - take risks here
☐ Moderate danger area - take calculated risks
▨ High danger area - take no risks

Figure 2.11   Relative safety and danger areas of the field.

OVERHEAD PASS

This technique, also called a flick, is useful for defenders looking to clear a congested area. It is used more frequently and successfully in the men's game because of the overall body strength required, but there is more to this skill than brute strength. Timing and coordination are critical. The technique requires that you have the ball further in front of your body and that you have your body lower than you would if you were pushing the ball. Transfer your weight as in a push pass (in the direction of your target).

Matthew Wells, a deep defender in the Australian hockey team, The Kookaburras, is very good at this skill. The following are his tips and comments for developing the overhead pass:

- Get low to the ground by bending your knees.
- Place the ball in the correct position in front of your body.
- Rotate through the hips.

- Be realistic, and keep your expectations within your own limits. Don't try to throw the ball too far!
- Basically, the body position and motion are the same as when you're pushing the ball, but the idea is to get under the ball to create more leverage and get the necessary elevation.
- When you are starting out, it is much easier to execute the skill from a dead-ball situation than with a rolling ball. When you get better at throwing overheads, try to execute the skill with the moving ball. In this instance it is better if the ball is moving forward (not sideways or across the line that your body weight is moving), as it will make it easier to pick the ball up on your stick. Also, that small forward momentum can give the ball an extra few yards of flight.
- Position the ball out in front of you so that you step into the ball and can get underneath it to get the lift required. This ball position also allows you to get the rotation you need through the hips, which will give you the required distance and power.

If the ball is too close to your body, you will be cramped and rely on your arms alone to perform the skill. If the ball is too far in front of your body, you will reach for the ball and won't be able to get the leverage required or the full hip rotation. In this situation it will be difficult to get the ball in the air. The distance you can cover with this skill will come largely from power generated through the rotation of your hips, not so much from the arms (although they do play a part). The lower to the ground you can get your body, the greater the power you will generate from the rotation.

The ability to throw a long overhead pass is an important skill to have, whether you use it to relieve pressure in deep defence if the opposition forwards have you pressed in, or to throw the ball from one side of the field to the other into space because the opposition is pressing to one side but leaving plenty of space behind the press. It is also quite handy to be able to throw short overheads over a single player for a team-mate to run onto or over an opposition line (the striker line of players or the midfield line) so that one pass eliminates multiple players.

Your ability to make effective passes to your team-mates will make you a valuable team player. There are many passing techniques, and each serves its purpose—whether that be power, subtlety, loft or speed of execution. The pressure that is applied by your direct opponent and your relative positioning on the field will also be a factor when choosing a technique for passing the ball. You need to maximise your repertoire of passing techniques so that you keep your passing options open. This will keep your opponents guessing, give you more penetration in your pass and allow you more time for the skill's execution.

☐ **CHAPTER 3** ☐

DRIBBLING

If you measured the amount of time you actually have in possession of the ball during a game, it would be very little (maybe as little as a minute or two), so when you do have control of the ball, you want to make the most of it.

When you are looking to improve your ability to move with the ball and get maximum benefit for your possession, consider several principles:

• **Keep it simple.** Keep the ball in one position as much as you can so you avoid moving it from side to side unnecessarily. If the ball does not need to move from a safe and comfortable position in front of you, don't complicate your movement by diverting your attention to unnecessary stick and ball contacts.

• **Stay tight.** Except in situations in which you can afford to toss the ball ahead and run onto it, keep your stick in touch with the ball and minimise the 'tic-tac' sound that your stick makes when you move the ball from one side to the other. The really good players move the ball quietly because the stick doesn't leave the surface of the ball when they are changing the direction of the ball. When you use this tactic, it is difficult for opponents to steal possession without fouling, and you have a better feel for where the ball is positioned while looking ahead and assessing your options. Also, you may choose to make a push pass, and this option will take less time to execute and will be more deceptive if you already have your stick on the ball.

In a tight situation in which you are surrounded by opponents, team-mates or even the sideline, you need to keep the ball very close to the end of your stick. This tight dribbling technique allows you to protect the ball, eliminate players and manoeuvre yourself into a better position to continue dribbling or to make a pass. (See figure 3.1.)

When you are in space, perhaps in a breakaway situation in the midfield, you can afford to throw the ball ahead and run onto it. This will allow you to run at greater speed.

31

Figure 3.1 Keep the ball tight on your stick as you move and hold the ball in a position so that you can scan ahead.

This loose dribbling style also gives you an opportunity to get your head up and see what is going on around you so that you improve your peripheral vision.

• **Stay strong.** You need to be strong over the ball when you are dribbling. You have worked hard to gain possession, so you will want to protect the ball from the opposition when you have it. The lower your right hand is down the stick, the stronger you will be with the ball, but strength sometimes comes at a price. If your right hand is too low, you may lose vision of your surroundings. Unless you bend your knees (this is hard to do at speed), your focus will be lower to the ground, but sometimes this sacrifice of vision for strength is necessary. You may assume this strong position to slow the play and hold possession without looking to gain significant territory as you wait for a team-mate to make good position, or you may try to force the opposition to foul you, and then you can win a free hit.

• **Maintain your peripheral vision.** This allows you to see available options in the distance when you are in possession of the ball. You need to be able to see the options your team-mates are creating for you, and good peripheral vision will allow you to make better decisions about your use of the ball. When players are tired, stressed or nervous, peripheral vision is one of the first components of their game to disappear. Often you will see players 'overplaying' the ball with their head down, or holding onto the ball too long as a result of a lack of peripheral vision. If you don't have good peripheral vision, you will miss the good options upfield, and the players around might become so frustrated that they stop leading and no longer make themselves available to you as a passing option.

14   CONTROL AND DART

Purpose

To improve your ability to move with the ball so that it is in position for you to change direction quickly while maintaining your peripheral vision.

Procedure

One player holds up numbers (or fingers) while you and the other players run towards him. If you're running with the ball you must call out the numbers you see as you are moving with the ball. The player leading the drill can also point left and right so that the other players change direction according to the directions they see in their peripheral vision.

• **Change lines.** Hockey is largely a game of manipulating angles. When I talk about changing lines, I mean altering the direction of movement so as to change the angle on which you are moving with the ball relative to your opponent or your goal. (See figure 3.2.) By changing your angles, you change the nature of the immediate playing environment. This creates new passing options for you and makes the opponents reassess their defensive options.

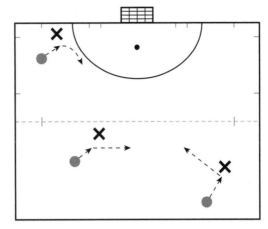

Figure 3.2 Changing lines.

In this way you can also eliminate opponents from the immediate contest by cutting the chasing player's line. As the player with the ball, if you change the line on which you move so as to move across your opponent's line of movement, the opposition player needs to readjust her line and pace of movement, which gives you more time to execute the next skill. This makes tackling and dispossessing you a more difficult task for your opponent.

15   DRIBBLE AND CUT

Purpose

To improve your ability to recognise when to cut the line of another player and to demonstrate how effective this is in eliminating the chasing player from the contest.

Procedure

In pairs, take turns running with the ball. With the ball, the first player starts running ahead of the second player, who chases from behind. You (the ball carrier) cut left and right to 'cut' the line of the chasing player, thereby eliminating the chasing player from each contest. Swap roles.

The ability to move with the ball with confidence and strength is a critical part of the game. It is tempting to carry the ball for too long and overlook passes, so a balance between the passing and dribbling skills is required. Each dribbling technique serves a purpose, and you must develop each of these to give yourself a greater number of options when you have the ball according to the space you have available to you.

The transition from trapping to moving with the ball and ultimately making a pass is important, so make sure you receive the ball in the optimal carrying position, and carry the ball in the best passing position as you move with it according to your surroundings. You should always try to carry the ball in a strong passing position; it just so happens that this position (with the ball in front of your body and in front of your right foot) is also the position in which you carry the ball to move quickly with maximum vision.

Alyson Annan, considered by many to be the best female player ever to play the game, is an outstanding dribbler. Luciana Aymar, a midfielder for Argentina, is another very strong dribbler. One of their strengths is that they can accelerate with the ball almost as quickly as they can without the ball—very fast!

The three basic dribbling techniques are straight, Indian, and reverse.

STRAIGHT DRIBBLE

You can use this method when you want to move over the ground at any speed. You carry the ball on your forestick, and if you are running quickly, you simply knock the ball a small distance ahead of you as you run if you have space to move into.

Alternatively, you can keep the ball tight on the end of your stick, which will make it more difficult for your opponent to make a successful tackle. But, if you have a lot of space, you can afford to throw the ball further ahead of you (sometimes called the 'loose dribble') and run onto it. In this way you are likely to be able to travel more quickly than you can with the ball in tight possession, and you can scan ahead for your next option or obstacle. The straight dribble is a good technique to use for carrying the ball if you want to travel over the ground quickly while at the same time maximising your vision and assessing your options.

16   DRIBBLING RELAY

Purpose

To practice dribbling the ball in a controlled manner at speed.

Procedure

If you have four players or more that need to practice this skill, set up teams for a relay. Vary the distance over which the relay will operate (10 metres to 40 metres, or 33 feet to 130 feet), and make sure that the ball is controlled at all times. You can vary the extent to which you must execute a tight or loose dribble, but you must demonstrate control of the ball at all times and must stop the ball before the next player can take off with it.

17   DRIBBLE AND PROTECT

Purpose

To introduce the practical side of dribbling by protecting the ball as you move with it while maintaining your vision and control of the ball.

Procedure

To practice a tight dribble, set up an area in which you and all the other players move with a ball each. (Start with a large area such as a quarter of the field, and make the area smaller to increase the level of difficulty.) Move with the balls in the confined area (vary the size of the confined area) while maintaining vision off the ball. While moving with and protecting your own ball, knock other players' balls out of the area when you have the opportunity. When you have your ball knocked out of the area, you are out of the game. The last remaining player is the winner.

INDIAN DRIBBLE

This technique is more complicated than the straight dribble, and as a result it diverts your attention from the positional changes of the players around you. Your peripheral vision can suffer because you need to pay close attention to each contact with the ball.

The Indian dribble allows you to change direction by moving the ball from left to right and right to left as required.

Your left hand remains at the top of the stick and does most of the physical work (it is tight on the top of the stick as for most of the skills of the game), while your right hand is looser and allows your left hand to rotate the stick within it. In this way you can move the ball from your forestick side to your reverse stick and back again to change direction and eliminate opponents. As is usually the case in the game of hockey, your left arm needs to be strong because it moves the weight of the stick, whereas the right hand plays more of a supporting role and fine-tunes the movements of the stick.

Quite often, left-handers are good hockey players because they are strong on the left side. So, when they complain about the fact that there are no left-handed sticks, suggest to them that perhaps all sticks are left-handed and in fact there are no right-handed sticks for the rest of us! (See figure 3.3.)

Figure 3.3 Hold the stick firmly with your left hand and allow the stick to move within your looser right hand.

18 DRAG COUNTER

Purpose

To improve your control of the ball as you move it from side to side with speed.

Equipment

One stick, one ball.

Procedure

Mark a distance of a stick's length on the ground. Move the ball across this distance (all the way to the markers) slowly at first, and gradually build up speed. Count the number of movements between the markers that you can achieve in a given time (30 seconds or 1 minute), and try to increase this with each attempt.

19 OBSTACLE BOX

Purpose

To improve your ability to change direction using the Indian dribbling technique while maintaining good vision.

Procedure

Set up obstacles in a confined area. You and other players move in that area, but you must avoid each other and the obstacles. To move around another player or an obstacle, you must use this Indian dribbling technique to change direction. Reduce the size of the area and increase the number of obstacles to make the drill more difficult and to introduce the need for faster movements. As in the earlier drill, you can knock other players' balls out of play.

REVERSE DRIBBLE

With the use of the reverse dribble, you can carry the ball wide on your left side and position your body to protect the ball from an opponent on your right or slightly behind you on your right. Be careful not to obstruct your opponent, but if you continue to move on the same line, this should not be a problem. Once again, you will need strength in your left hand and arm, as your right hand will not be in contact with the stick. Rather, it will help to balance your body as you run.

Make sure you maintain your vision off the ball and use this technique only when necessary, because it is difficult to run at speed with the ball out wide on the left side of your body. It is also a weak position in which to hold the ball, and it is difficult to make an effective pass from this position. You might use the reverse dribble during your initial take-off when you earn or steal possession, or if you are travelling along the left sideline and need to protect the ball from an opposition player.

As soon as you have space, return the ball to a more comfortable and safer position on your forestick, which will give you greater strength over the ball and the ability to run at greater speed. It will also open up passing options for you. (See figure 3.4.)

Figure 3.4 Carry the ball on your left side, wide of your body and use your right arm to balance for maximum strength.

20   LEFT-HAND JOG AND RELAY

Purpose

To improve your ability to control the ball using only the left hand.

Procedure

Begin by jogging across the field with the ball outside the left side of your body and your stick in your left hand. Do this until you are comfortable in this position, then speed up as you get better at controlling the ball. You can set up a relay competition, as in the other dribbling techniques. As always, you must control the ball at all times, even if you tap it slightly ahead.

21   LEFT-HAND JOG AND CHANGE

Purpose

To improve your ability to control the ball on your left side so that when time permits you can quickly move it into a stronger position. It will also improve the strength of your left arm and require the use of peripheral vision.

Procedure

As you move across the field with the ball on the left, a spare player or coach raises a hand, at which point you move the ball from your left to the stronger right-hand side. Once you have the ball controlled on the forestick, move the ball back to the reverse side while still travelling at some speed, and continue following the instructions of the person giving the signals.

22   LEFT-HAND STEAL

Purpose

To improve your ability to steal the ball using your left hand only, explode out of the contest with the ball and get the ball into position to make a good pass.

Equipment

Five to eight balls

Procedure

Place the balls on a sideline. Begin a couple of metres in front of the line and move quickly towards the ball as though you were stealing possession or collecting a loose ball in the field of play. Take possession of the ball with your stick in your left hand, and accelerate off the line with the ball. Once you are moving forward with the ball, transfer the ball to your forestick side and make a pass to a target. This will simulate a game situation. Again, this could be a relay situation.

23   LEFT-ARM TAP

Purpose

To improve the strength of your left arm.

Procedure

Practice tapping the ball on the toe of your stick using your left hand to control the stick. Begin by positioning your left hand low on the stick, and move it towards the top of the stick as you get stronger. Count the number of taps that you can do without dropping the ball to the ground, and look to increase that number each time.

All players need to carry the ball with confidence and speed. In each game instance, the technique chosen will depend upon the space available and the subsequent intended action such as a pass, goal shot or elimination skill. Keep your dribbling style simple to minimize unnecessary contacts with the ball. Change your angles of movement to maximize your strength over the ball.

☐ CHAPTER 4 ☐

LEADING

No matter which position you play, you need to develop strong leading skills to help you get in good position to receive the ball from your team-mates. This will give you the opportunity to implement the other skills of the game. Leading is an important skill that requires significant awareness of your surroundings and some planning of your next move.

Much of your time on the field is spent leading, so you need to be good at it. But there will be times when you feel your leads, despite their quality, are being ignored by your team-mates.

Lead infield and cut across the line of the ball when you have the opportunity so that you receive the ball in the most dangerous (central) area of the field. In this way you will have the best possible angle to run at the circle or at an isolated defender, and you reduce the number of opponents you need to confront and the distance to the circle. By leading for the ball with this ultimate positioning in mind, you will also increase your options for your next movement (you won't be restricted by the sideline). This will all make it more difficult for your opponent to tackle you effectively.

GETTING THE BALL

Getting the ball is not the only objective of your game. So, unless you believe you are in good position to improve the ball position for your team, be careful that you don't demand the ball just for the sake of it.

If you demand the ball in situations that won't place the ball in an improved position, your good and appropriate leads might be overlooked down the track. Just as the boy who cried wolf was ignored because he was always demanding attention, your leads will start to be overlooked if you demand the ball all the time and you are not in good position to be doing so. You will be better served to make good leads at appropriate times and strongly demand it with your voice only when you believe you present a really good option.

If you watch and play enough hockey, you will see examples of players continuously screaming for the ball and leading selfishly simply to chalk up individual possessions.

KEY NOTE
Remember that a lead can be a deliberate attempt to distract the opposition, so you do not need to get the ball every time for your lead to be effective.

39

Magdalena Aicega of Argentina is challenged by Mijntje Donners of the Netherlands.

This is not in the best interest of the team! You will do better if you demand the ball only when you are in a really good position to receive the ball.

It's easy to become frustrated (particularly if you are a striker) when you make a lead that you think is a good one but it is ignored. Understand that the player with the ball has made the decision he or she thinks is best, and there may be a better option that you are unable to see.

Keep leading, and eventually the ball will be delivered to you in good position. Always be ready (keep your stick low, focus on the play and be aware of the positioning of the players around you) so that when you do get the ball, you are well placed to take advantage of your opportunity. Also, consider that it is very difficult to maintain good peripheral vision in the midfield and in deep defence. Players with the ball in these positions are often surrounded by several opponents, and their focus needs to be entirely on the ball as a result. In these tight situations these players with the ball cannot necessarily be looking ahead of the play at the critical moment when you are making your lead, so your timing is crucial and patience is necessary. Congested situations are part and parcel of the position that midfielders play, and even the best ball carriers will not see some leads further up the field. Don't take it personally!

On the other hand, it is worth talking to the players who deliver the ball to you to check that they see your leads as an option. If they do not see your leads, explain what you are trying to do (perhaps at half-time or after the game), and draw their attention to this at training. In training, practice leading and receiving from the players around you; this will help everybody. Over time, players will learn more about the leading styles (and passing abilities) of their team-mates, and confusion will be reduced.

If the other players are seeing your leads and choosing not to pass to you, talk to them about their reasons for that. As we will discuss later, communication on and off the field is important, so be sure to make your points in a positive manner and be careful to listen to what your team-mates have to say. You might learn something!

Because of the fluid nature of the game, there is often a lot of noise on the playing field and very little time between passes and actions. You may not be able to communicate with your voice where you want the ball. So you must use your body and your stick to be demonstrative with your lead.

If you watch elite players, usually those who lead at the right time with sharp definition and certainty earn the highest number of possessions. Obviously, this is not a true measure of their value to the team, but it gives them more opportunity to make a difference, and it gives a confident message to the players passing the ball.

The timing of your lead is critical. You need to be aware of your team-mate's readiness to make the pass. If you lead when your team-mate is not ready or not in good position to see your lead and make the necessary pass, the lead may well be wasted and a good offensive opportunity will be lost.

MAKING THE LEAD

All field players need to make leads. Strikers make leads of all lengths while midfielders and defenders usually make shorter, sharper leads because they operate in a congested area of the field more often. The following are some tips for making great leads.

Change the Pace

The quality of a lead is often determined by a change of pace. By changing the pace of your lead, you will catch your opponents unaware and make them react to your movement rather than dictate it. If they are forced to react to you, then you have the advantage of some extra time in which to receive the ball in a strong position, away from the contest.

A lead can be as simple as a sharp movement of the stick, but often a change in pace determines the ultimate success of the lead. Usually, it is acceleration that constitutes a lead. In this instance you might appear disinterested in the play before accelerating sharply, catching your immediate opponent unaware and leaving him or her flat-footed and reacting to your latest move. You now have a small break on your opponent and can receive the ball with some space. This can happen over a short distance or over a longer distance.

A sharp deceleration can work just as effectively. In this instance, you and your opponent might both be running at full speed before the leading player slows down suddenly, leaving the opposition player running at the same pace. The player reacting to the lead overruns the play, and the leading player can receive the ball with time and space. You aren't likely to eliminate your opponent in this manner (they will probably still be ahead of you), but you will buy yourself some time to receive the ball with space, change your line of movement and reassess your options.

Give Your Team-Mate a Target

You need to give your team-mates a target. Use your stick as a pointer. This communicates to the player making the pass exactly where you want to receive the ball, and it is particularly useful in tight and noisy situations.

Keep your stick on the ground where it is most easily visible to the player with the ball, because he will most often have his head down as he moves with the ball. A sharp movement of the stick can also catch the attention of the ball carrier, whose focus may be narrow in tight, congested situations (see figure 4.1).

When you are leading over any distance, the definite placement of your stick shows the person delivering the ball exactly where you want to receive the ball in relation to

Figure 4.1 Make your lead a definite one. Keep your stick low to the ground and make it a clear target for the player passing the ball.

your body. In this situation you can avoid the need to change the pace at which you run to react to the pass because the ball can be delivered to the perfect position for you.

If a team-mate makes a pass that is only vaguely in your direction, you may have to slow down or speed up to receive and control the ball, which can disrupt your plans for the next move. You can receive the ball while running at the ideal speed for your next movement by using your stick to give the player passing the ball a clear target.

24   EYE CATCHER

Purpose

To demonstrate the need to make an eye-catching movement when you are leading, particularly when the player delivering the ball is under pressure. If the player delivering the ball doesn't see your lead, you probably won't receive the ball.

Procedure

Create a competitive practice environment so that two, three or four players begin in a similar position. These players (A, B, C and so on) lead for the ball, and player D (the ball carrier) makes a pass to the player who best attracts his or her attention. That player shoots at goal (use a goalkeeper if possible). In this drill the timing and sharpness of the lead are critical. Do this 10 times and then determine which player is leading the possession count and why that is. Swap positions and do the same exercise over and over again. Introduce another player (player E) into the drill to apply pressure to player D, which will require players A to C to be demonstrative with their leads to attract the attention of player D, who is under pressure. Player E makes a pass to player D, then applies pressure to player D, who must look for a lead by a player upfield. Player D makes a pass to the first player (A, B or C and so on) who attracts his or her attention.

25   JOG AND LEAD

Purpose

To practice each of the leading alternatives.

Procedure

Jog beside the ball carrier. The carrier makes a pass according to the predetermined lead in the form of a sharp stick movement, a change of pace or a sharp body movement.

Relead

Releading is critical. We have already discussed the frustrating nature of the leading game, so you will by now appreciate that you need to master the art of releading if you are to regularly get the ball on the end of your stick—and maintain your sanity!

The first lesson to learn is that rarely is your first lead rewarded with the ball. Often the first couple of leads are fakes used to set your opponent up in a position that will make it difficult for him or her to prevent you from getting the ball. It might be your third or fourth lead that represents your genuine intention to get the ball. In this situation you need to think a couple of steps ahead and manipulate your opponent s position so that you can lead into the best position for your next move according to the position of the player passing the ball. On the other hand, you may be ignored on your first couple of genuine leads, and you will need to relead if you are to continue presenting as an option and making space for your team-mates.

26   LEAD COORDINATION AND 2-ON-1

Purpose

To practice leading when the player carrying the ball is ready to make a pass.

Procedure

Player A moves through a set of cones with the ball. Player B (vary the distance between passer and receiver) has an opponent and must move or lead within a confined area to momentarily lose that player. The leads must be timed according to the readiness of the ball carrier to make the pass (when player A is through the set of cones). Player A passes according to the lead and the target that is provided

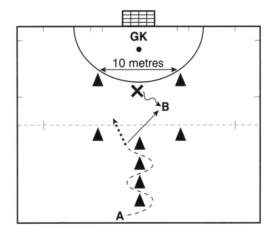

Figure 4.2 Lead coordination 2-on-1.

by player B and joins in the attack to create a 2-on-1 situation against the defender. Player B needs to try moving the defender out of the area that she ultimately wants to receive the ball in, and relead as appropriate according to the readiness of the player delivering the ball (player A). If the defender starts to anticipate (cheat!), or if player B can't get away to receive the ball, then player A can continue forward to create a 2-on-1 situation in the confined area. The attackers shoot at goal when they get into the circle. (See figure 4.2.)

Lead Over Longer Distances

Strikers need to develop leading skills for all situations. Much of your time as a forward is spent manipulating your defender or your immediate opponent into a position that gives you an advantage when receiving the ball.

Usually the strikers become the most frustrated with the leading process because the ball carriers seem to overlook or ignore their leads. Usually several good options are closer to the ball carriers and are easier for them to see. Also, strikers are often discouraged from chasing the ball or hunting for it downfield when their leads are not rewarded with the ball, because that creates increased congestion in the midfield and leaves fewer options available in attack for later in the play. They are very much at the mercy of other team-mates when it comes to earning possession and for this reason, strikers sometimes feel they are not involved enough in the game. Keep leading, and you will get your opportunity!

You know you are leading well when you hear the defenders making confused and panicked calls at each other. Not only are they uncertain of their individual roles, but their attention is also divided among you, the ball, their team-mates and their relative positioning. They are distracted, and in this time you can make a quick break into space. Perfect!

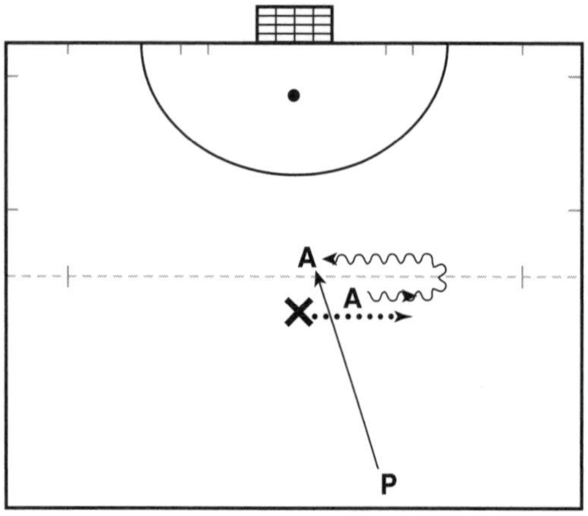

As a striker, you may receive a long pass from a deep defender that is hit 40 to 50 metres (44 to 55 yards). If you time your lead well and remember to relead (don't think that one lead is enough), you can receive while moving towards your goal in space and with a break on your immediate opponent. (See figure 4.3.)

The other frustrating part of leading when the ball needs to travel a long distance to get to you is that you rely on almost perfect passing execution by your team-mate, and there is more time for something to go wrong. Your opponents might make an interception or get a touch on the ball to make a deflection, which throws off the timing of your lead and changes the trajectory of the ball. And over a longer distance more opponents can interfere with the ball.

Despite the risks involved, the pass over a long distance can be the most penetrating and damaging of them all because it can eliminate many opponents at one time, and it often gives the receiving player an opportunity to receive in a position that has the immediate defender in an isolated position.

Figure 4.3 Moving a defender out of space.

KEY NOTE
When you are leading, anticipate the ideal receiving position and take your opponent away from that area so that you can lead into it when the time is right. Usually that will mean trying to receive in the most central position possible.

Lead When the Ball Is Close

Many of the principles of leading already discussed are relevant in tighter situations also, but there are some differences that are significant in congested positions such as the midfield, deep defence or the attacking circle. Leading in these areas needs to be particularly short, sharp and definitive.

As discussed already, you need to use your stick as a target for the player delivering the ball, and you need to lead over and over again. It is perhaps more critical to make a clear target in the congested areas than the non-congested areas of the field because there is less space in which to move, and decision-making time is such a rarity. Also, there is no margin for passing error in tight situations.

Often you will lead to draw opposition players away from your team-mate with the ball rather than to receive the ball yourself. In this tight situation, you must keep your stick low to the ground because the situation may quickly change and you will need to react quickly to the pass that may be made to you in an unexpected position.

If you wave your stick around in the air, not only is the target a vague one, but the ball carrier may not take it seriously because you don't look ready to receive. Also, you will need extra time to get your stick into position to make a good trap. This is critical in congested and tightly-contested situations.

Drift Away From the Defender

This drifting technique is useful if you are running close to your team-mate who has the ball. At the last second you can drift to the right (or left as appropriate), across the face of the opponent who is marking you. In so doing you can create some important space for yourself as you receive the ball, and the opponent will need to adjust his positioning.

The drifting technique is a variation on a 2-on-1 situation whereby the player without the ball appears to be running at pace with the team-mate, then slows down and drifts wide. Not only are you far enough from your defender to receive the ball with time, but the defender (now off his line) will take time to react to your deceleration, and there will be more space for you to move into at speed. (See figure 4.4.)

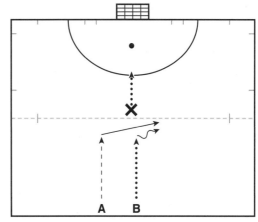

Figure 4.4 Drift away from the defender.

27 DRIFT AWAY AND SHOOT

Purpose

To practice leading away from the ball (in both directions).

Procedure

Players A and B pass the ball through the cones as they move towards goal. At the last cone, player A leads away from the ball with a quick dynamic movement and then receives the ball from player B and shoots at goal. Player B follows in for the rebound. Alternate sides so that the players practice this drifting away leading technique on both sides of their body—they need to receive on both their flat and reverse-stick sides. (See figure 4.5.)

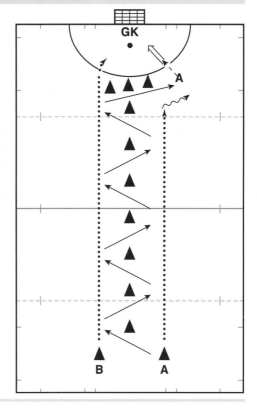

Figure 4.5 Drift away and shoot.

Readjust Your Position

When the ball is in defence or deep midfield, strikers constantly need to readjust their offensive positions, even though the ball will not necessarily be delivered to them. This movement and the subsequent manipulation of the defenders will create space for other players on your team to use and move into, and it will also create space for you to lead into when you are ready to receive the ball. At the same time you will keep the defenders on their toes and somewhat distracted from their other tasks.

As a forward, you can create confusion for your opponent by moving continuously and readjusting your position. High strikers use this technique to create good leading and receiving opportunities. You can do this by moving continually between your opponent and your attacking goal so that the defender must turn his or her attention from the live play upfield to your movement behind.

When the time is right and your defender appears comfortable with your position and seems to know where you are situated and has his or her attention focused back on the play, you can make another lead behind, which forces a division of attention once again. You may not receive the ball in this situation, but you might distract your opponent sufficiently so that your team-mates can capitalise on that distraction. The skill for the defender is to be positioned so as to minimise the extent to which she needs to turn her head from the action. The best position will be one in which she can see both the live play and the movement of the opponent.

If your defender continues to watch you in isolation, he can't watch the play simultaneously, which means the attacker (who is able to watch the upcoming play) can read the play better than the opponent and get away with a break into space at his convenience. All players lead for the ball during a game, and in doing so they attempt to receive the ball with minimal interference from their opponents. The better the lead, the more space you afford yourself to receive the ball and make your next move.

A good lead will have your opponent reacting to your move, which immediately puts you in a position of strength. But the extent to which this occurs will be determined by a combination of timing, definition, conviction and tone, sharpness, target provided and change of pace of the lead. A lead can be in the form of a quick flick of the stick or a 40-metre plus (44-yard) sprint across or up the field. Almost certainly you will need to relead if you are to maximise your involvement in the game.

☐ CHAPTER 5 ☐

TACKLING AND INTERCEPTING

If you are making a tackle or trying to intercept the ball, then you are trying to get the ball from opposition players. All players need to be able to tackle, but obviously the defenders are the experts—as they are usually very good at reminding the rest of us!

Midfielders and strikers usually win possession by making clever interceptions and by stealing the ball with an unexpected tackle. In combination with the traditional tackling techniques, these possession-winning alternatives (sneaky steals and interceptions) make up an important element of the game, which will help you earn possession. Of course, your team will benefit if you force turnovers by the opposition and minimise your own.

An important part of dispossessing the opposing team is your ability to anticipate the movement of the ball and get to it first to make an interception. The players who 'read the play' well generally get to the ball first and make timely interceptions, earning many possessions over the course of the game. You improve your chances of making a tackle or a clean interception if you read the play successfully, because your preparation will be improved. Often this subtle ability comes through match experience and accumulated game time.

The keys to making a good tackle are getting low to the ground (particularly in the defensive circle), mobility, patience for the best tackling opportunity, strength and the ability to use a variety of tackling options. Also, as a tackler you can be proactive and manipulate the ball carrier (rather than the other way round), by channelling him into a position that is best for you as a tackler to make your move.

28   1-ON-1S

Purpose

To improve your ability to dispossess your opponent in a tight situation.

Procedure

Mark an area 10 metres by 5 metres (33 feet by 16 feet) using one of the sidelines or the entry into the goal circle to make the drill more realistic. If you cannot use the circle area, mark a line that will be used as a goal at one end of the designated drill area. The player with the ball runs at the tackler, attempting to dribble the ball over the line to score a goal. The tackler must make a clean tackle using any of the appropriate tackling techniques. The drill can become more competitive as necessary so that the players keep score of the successful tackles and the number of goals scored by the ball carrier. Vary the size of the playing area to introduce different tackling techniques. You can also move the drill to any position around the outside of the circle so that the defenders must channel the attacker into a less dangerous situation and the forwards can shoot at goal from various angles if they win the contest. This drill is the best way to practice all the tackling techniques. The particular technique chosen will depend on the part of the field you use for the drill and also the speed, control and skills of the player with the ball.

29   CONTINUOUS 1-ON-1S

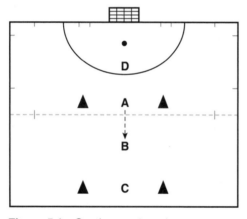

Figure 5.1   Continuous 1-on-1s.

Purpose

To practice tackling techniques in a fluid situation.

Procedure

Player A attacks in a 1-on-1 situation with player B. If player A beats player B and then he passes to player C, then player A becomes the defender against player C. If player B dispossesses player A, then he (player B) passes to player D, and player A becomes the defender with player D now attacking. Continue in this manner using as many players as you like. (See figure 5.1.)

CHANNELLING THE PLAYER

Olympic gold medallist Matthew Wells has significant strength when it comes to tackling and channelling players. This is what he has to say about the art of channelling the player with the ball as well as tackling:

The idea is to dictate to the attacker where you want him or her to move with the ball, not the other way around. This action is known as channelling the player with the ball, and it gives you maximum control of the contested situation. When you're channelling players, it is best to be able to push them wide to the sidelines or to the backline, but when you are caught in the middle of the field, you generally want to force the ball carrier onto your forestick or onto the forestick of a team-mate. The forestick is your strong side, and the opponent's reverse-stick side is her weaker side. If you channel the player with the ball onto your forestick, she will be forced to carry the ball on her reverse-stick side.

TACKLING

When making a tackle in a situation whereby the play has slowed down or is in a confined area, you must be able to get low to the ground and get your stick flat on the ground so that you cover a bigger area. In this way you can protect your feet and avoid giving away a free hit, but at the same time you need to remain mobile by not having your feet 'planted' to the ground. If you are eliminated in this situation, you can still recover quickly and stay in the contest.

In open-play situations where you are chasing an opponent, you need to be very patient as you prepare to make a tackle. Make your move when you are in the best possible position, or channel the player onto one of your better-placed team-mates. If you commit to the tackle

'Channelling gives you maximum control of the contested situation.'—Matthew Wells

too early, it can provide an easy elimination opportunity for the ball carrier.

Your mobility and ability to change direction are important, but the ability to channel the player wide or onto a team-mate is also an important skill in this situation. This will slow down the play and give you and your team-mates the opportunity to reposition and set up for a planned and coordinated attack on the ball carrier.

If you are not in good position to tackle, you can also choose simply to hold up the play by looking clumsy by getting your body or your feet in the way of the ball and 'accidently' giving away a free hit. The clumsy technique might be most useful in the midfield or in high attack, and it is considered an effective means of tackling or stopping the play while your team-mates catch up to the player with the ball and regroup. Be very careful about which part of the ground you do this in, as a clumsy tackle or a professional foul in the defensive 25-yard zone will result in a penalty corner for your opponent. This would be a last resort!

When you are contesting the ball in the defensive circle, remember that often the attacker is just looking to win a penalty corner if he cannot get a good shot away. There-fore, you need to anticipate this and protect your feet at all costs. Get low, keep your stick flat on the ground and remain mobile while keeping a good distance from the ball. You are an appropriate distance from the ball carrier if you can reach the ball with your stick outstretched because in this situation you also have time to move out of the way if the forward tries to force an obstruction or knock the ball onto your foot in the circle to win a penalty corner.

When making a tackle, do so with strength and purpose. Don't allow an attacker to bust through the tackle easily. A (quiet and unofficial) philosophy of many defenders is 'either the player gets past or the ball does, but never both!' Overall, balance, timing and strength are the most important elements of tackling, but the following factors are critical to making strong, reliable and legal tackles:

- Be balanced as you prepare to make the tackle.
- Ensure that your footwork is sharp to set up your body in a good position. Usually you will want to get into a 'side-on' position.
- Be mobile. This means that you can react quickly if the ball carrier changes direction. If you are mobile, your footwork will get your body into a side-on position so that your feet are not square with the approaching player. If your feet are square in this manner, you are likely to be flat-footed and slow to react to a change in your opponent's direction or pace.
- Keep your stick low at all times.
- Be proactive and channel your opponent so as to create the best position for you or a team-mate to make a tackle.
- Be alert and ready to pounce on your tackling opportunity when it arrives.
- Keep your weight on the balls of your feet. Avoid being in a flat-footed position and having your feet in a square position as the player with the ball approaches. (See figure 5.2.)

Figure 5.2 Ready to make a tackle: mobile, one foot in front of the other, weight on your toes and stick low to the ground.

Poke

The poke tackle is a technique used when your opponent momentarily loses control of the ball. This usually occurs in fluid play at moments when the ball spills loose or your opponent takes her stick off the ball while making a pass or a goal shot. At the moment that the ball is left unprotected, you need to be ready to 'poke' your stick at the ball to remove it from your opponent's control.

Your intention may not be to win possession for yourself, but you will stop the momentum of the attacker and create a loose-ball contested situation if you poke the ball away from the player with the ball. This might also give your team-mates an opportunity to jump on the spillage and win possession.

You can also make a dummy tackle before you are ready to execute the real thing, which will take the attention of the ball carrier away from his control of the ball. It also makes the player with the ball respond to you rather than you responding to the ball carrier.

In a poke tackle your body position is usually side-on with one foot in front of the other, but often this tackle is useful in tight situations in which you are not well balanced. If you intend only to knock the ball loose from the ball carrier and create another contest for other players, you may be able to execute this tackle sufficiently when you are off balance or do not have the ideal footwork. (See figure 5.3.)

KEY NOTE
Remember that to some extent as a tackler, you can be proactive and dictate the timing, movement and play of an opponent.

Figure 5.3 Get side-on and poke your stick at the ball when the ball carrier momentarily loses control of the ball. You may need to stretch to do this.

30   THE POKE

Purpose

To get comfortable with the poke technique.

Procedure

The player with the ball moves the ball from side to side in a stationary position. The tackler must assess the best time to make the poke tackle to knock the ball away from the attacker without hitting the attacker's stick.

Variation

The player with the ball jogs towards the defender and moves the ball from side to side as she moves. The defender must make a poke tackle at the right moment when the ball appears to be loose.

Figure 5.4 Keep left foot in front of right and low to the ground; lunge forward to the ball but don't overcommit.

Figure 5.5 Be strong in the flat tackle and slide your stick along the ground to maximise the distance you can cover.

Lunge

This tackling technique requires you to be in good position—ideally balanced, low to the ground, weight forward with your left foot in front of your right foot. Your left hand may be the only hand used if you are lunging and stretching a long way forward on your flat-stick side, so make sure that your timing is 'spot on' because, as the name suggests, you need to lunge forward and commit your weight and momentum to that movement. It may take time to recover and get back in the play if you are not successful on your first attempt. (See figure 5.4.) Don't eliminate yourself from the contest by overcommitting to the tackle.

Flat

This forestick technique is useful in a confined space such as tight midfield situations or in the defensive circle. Usually, the player with the ball moves the ball into your path because he has moved too close to you before making an elimination attempt. There is very little, if any, backswing involved; and your stick, which is strong and flat to the ground, covers a wide area. (See figure 5.5.)

31   LOW TACKLING IN THE CIRCLE

Purpose

To practice getting low to protect your feet and prevent giving away a penalty corner.

Procedure

Set up a 2-on-1 drill moving along the baseline in the circle or anywhere outside the circle. The attacker must try to knock the ball onto the foot of the defender or eliminate the defender entirely from the contest. The defender protects his feet and simultaneously tries to dispossess the player with the ball.

Flat-Reverse

For this technique you need a strong left hand because you probably will not be able to position your right hand on your stick without losing balance and reach.

With your left hand at the top of your stick and the point of the stick towards the ground, keep your stick low and in front of your body with the head of the stick forward of your left hand for increased strength. This slight forward angle of your stick will make it more difficult for the ball carrier to barge through your tackle. If your stick head is in front of your hand on the handle of the stick for this tackle, you will be in a stronger position if the player with the ball (who is carrying the ball on her strong forestick side) tries to force her way through the tackle.

Your stick should also be angled so that the top edge is forward of the bottom edge. In this way if the ball makes contact with your stick in the tackle, it will wedge between your stick and the surface of the field, which will make it easier for you to control and more difficult for your opponent to recover. (See figure 5.6.)

When you make the flat-reverse tackle you

Figure 5.6 Get low to the ground, have the toe of the stick forward of your left hand and the stick angled slightly forward towards the ground.

will be low to the ground and committed entirely to the contest. You will be slow to stand up again and chase if the player eliminates you, so be sure that you are likely to make a clean tackle or have adequate support from your team-mates around you who can pick up the pieces if you miss the tackle.

In our Olympic preparation we used cricket gloves on the left hand to practice this tackling technique, and we played lots of indoor hockey too. The gloves allow you to get your left hand to the ground to make the tackle without fear of sustaining an injury.

Reverse on the Run

This is not the perfect position for a defender to be in to make a tackle, but when you find yourself in that situation, run at least at the same speed as the ball carrier and with your stick in your left hand. When you are balanced, time your tackle for the moment when you think the ball carrier does not have good control of the ball, or when his attention and vision are averted.

Ultimately, the best opportunity in this situation may be to channel the ball carrier onto a team-mate who is in a better position to tackle (usually on his flat-stick side), or force him to the sideline in the same manner. You may also just knock the ball away from the ball carrier using this technique instead of making a tackle for possession.

Umpires are very tough on these reverse-side tackles, so unless you are sure you can get clean possession (there is no contact with the ball carrier's stick) or you just want to stop the play (a professional foul), you should be patient and channel the player into another contest.

KEY NOTE
Players all over the field can steal the ball, but usually a steal comes about when the player with the ball is not expecting—or is not aware that he is engaged in—a contest!

The Steal

This is really just another way of describing a tackle, but often it is a less orthodox technique that forwards often use as a possession earner. Forwards, for example, appear to come from nowhere at times and steal the ball from defenders.

The steal is usually a surprise for the player with the ball, and it most often comes about by a player chasing the ball carrier from behind and executing an unexpected tackle, which results in a turnover.

32   INTERCEPTING AND CALLING LINES

Purpose

To practice making sharp interceptions in a live situation with the help of a team-mate who is calling your line from behind.

Procedure

Player A tries to hit past player B to player C who is leading. Player D is calling the line for player B according to the movement of the leading player, player C. Player B cannot look behind but must rely solely upon the calls of his team-mate (player D). If player B intercepts the ball there is a 2v2 towards goal 1 (players B and D v A and C). If player A passes successfully to the leading player C, then it is a 2v2 to goal 2. (See figure 5.7.)

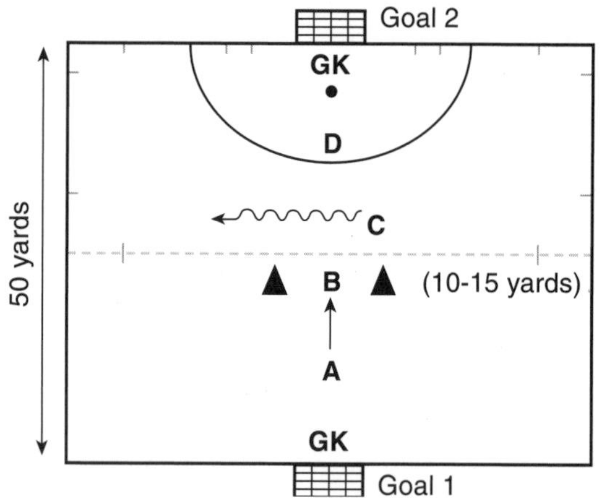

Figure 5.7 Intercepting and calling lines.

Tackling, channelling and intercepting are important components of the defensive game, and from these skills come exciting attacking opportunities. Rarely will you be in perfect position for each of the tackles that you make, but early preparation and concentration will increase the likelihood of this occurring through optimum balance and timing.

All players need to be able to execute the various tackling techniques; certainly the ability of all players to read the play and make interceptions (this comes through match experience) can make the difference for your team. Value your ability to channel players as a significant skill in itself. Although it may not be reflected on the stats sheet, these ball-winning skills might be the best action that you can take to help your team earn possession.

CHAPTER 6

DRAGS AND ELIMINATIONS

Drags and elimination skills allow you to change direction, create new angles of movement and eliminate opposition players as you move with the ball. These skills often look flashy and earn applause from spectators, but the appropriate use of them is a delicate balancing act. This will come about with match experience and a significant amount of trial and error.

As has already been discussed, keep your style of movement with the ball as simple as possible. This will minimise skill error and keep your attention focused on other necessary aspects for your movement and decision making, such as your peripheral vision. If your vision with the ball is good, it will allow you to make informed and early decisions about your next move. The principle of simplicity applies to the execution of your drags and elimination skills, which, in essence, are just more complicated ways of moving with the ball. You can drag left, right, try the toss and go, jink over an outstretched stick, or pass the ball around an opponent using the 2-on-1.

Every time you make a drag, you change the line on which you move, as discussed in chapter 3. You might be trying to get your opponent off balance to eliminate him from the immediate contest, or you may simply be trying to capitalise on his bad positioning by moving into available space.

DRAG LEFT

This is the technique for moving the ball from your right to your left. Move at your opponent's left leg (move to your right) and do your best to convince her that you will pass the ball to the right, or that you will keep moving in that direction. It may feel as though you are overacting, but this initial dummy will set you up to make the best of your drag to the left.

The idea is to use your body and weight transfer to convince your opponent that you are making a pass to your right and to get her to commit to that end. The timing of your next move is critical.

Watch the weight distribution of your opponent as he reacts to your dummy, and make your next move at exactly the right moment. At the moment that your opponent's weight commits to your right (because he thinks that you are passing that way or moving in that direction), pull the ball to your left. This movement needs to be quick and smooth, and ideally it requires your stick to remain on the ball. Make the drag move early. It is easy to find yourself getting too close to your opponent, which makes it easier for the opponent to interrupt your drag and dispossess you of the ball.

Basic Steps for the Drag Left

- Move towards the left foot of your opposition player as though to pass to her left (your right) or as though to continue moving in that direction.
- Having scanned your surroundings before you engage your opponent, watch for her commitment to your movement, dummy, or fake. Your opponent will transfer weight to the left (your right) when you have her 'sold' on the dummy, and she might also commit her stick to the left hand to try to make an interception of the anticipated pass.
- When she has committed her body weight to your dummy, make your move (drag left). Try to use a stick length as a guide, and begin your drag by the equivalent of this distance from your opponent. You will need to be ready to change your mind about your drag if the defender does not fall for the dummy, so don't try to execute the drag just because you planned to do so. You need to react to the defender's movement to some extent and reassess your options.
- With your stick tight on the ball, make your drag across the face of your opponent towards your left side. Try to make this move as square across the face of your opponent as possible so as to keep the ball away from the swinging stick and feet of your opponent.
- If you get around your opponent with this drag to the left, cut in behind to make sure she is eliminated from the contest so that you get maximum benefit for your clean skill execution.

You can practice the drag left in a confined area. Try to keep your stick on the ball all the time, which means there will be very little noise as you change the direction of the ball with your stick (figure 6.1).

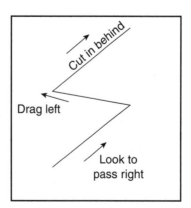

Figure 6.1 Drag left and cut.

33   DRAG LEFT

Purpose

To become comfortable with the technique of dragging the ball from right to left while keeping the stick on the ball.

Procedure

Use chalk to draw the diagram in figure 6.1 on a hard surface, or use cones to mark the shape on the ground. Practice moving the ball along the line, increasing the speed of the ball movement as you improve.

34   PASSIVE DRAG LEFT

Purpose

To introduce a live variable to the drag. The use of a passive defender requires the player with the ball to look for the appropriate cues to best execute this skill.

Procedure

Practice the drag left technique with a passive defender. Watch the defender who will commit to your dummy. At this time the player with the ball executes the drag as in the Drag Left drill. Ultimately, the passive defender will mix up the reactions so that on some occasions he will not be sold on the dummy, and the player with the ball will need to react to that by changing the move. As you get better at executing the skill slowly, increase the pace of your drag and the competitive nature of the drill so that ultimately the defender tries hard to dispossess the player with the ball. To keep the defender honest, move the ball right and continue in that direction so as to eliminate the defender on his reverse side instead.

DRAG RIGHT

The drag right is almost a mirror image of the drag left. No doubt you will find some drags and skills easier than others as you try to master the skills of the game. This drag was always the one that I needed to practice most diligently. For me it was always more natural to execute the drag left than the drag right, and I overused it so that my opponents began to anticipate my moves. But after lots of practice I was able to keep them guessing and execute both skills adequately.

Remember that when you discover your strengths in the game of hockey, you must be strong in the opposite skill or on the other side of your body. Otherwise, your opponents will anticipate your moves and you will lose that skill as a natural strength. Mix up hitting and pushing, dragging left and right, and placement of goal shots.

Basic Steps for the Drag Right

- Move towards the right foot of your opponent (your left).
- Make every effort to look as though you will continue moving left or make a pass to your opponent's right (that is, sell a dummy to your left). Sell the dummy using the transfer of your body weight to commit the defender to her right.
- Make your move early (approximately one stick length from your opponent), and watch for your opponent to commit her body weight to your movement left (her right).

KEY NOTE
Keep your opponents honest by bringing more and varied skills into your game, and you will always have your favourite and strongest skills up your sleeve when it is the right time to use them!

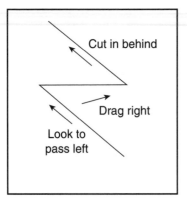

Figure 6.2 Drag right.

- Watch your opponent for a change in weight distribution and stick position. As soon as you think that your opponent is committed to your dummy, transfer the ball from your left foot to your right side, almost square across your opponent's body onto your forestick. (See figure 6.2.)
- Once you feel that you are past your opponent, cut in behind to eliminate her from the contest, as for the Drag Left drill.

35   DRAG RIGHT

Purpose

To become comfortable moving the ball to sell the dummy left and then drag it right.

Procedure

As for the drag left, draw the diagram in figure 6.2 on the ground and move the ball along the line. Increase the speed with which you do this as you improve and remember to practice your weight distribution. Introduce the passive defender as in the previous drill, and increase the competitiveness of the drill as appropriate. Keep the defender honest by occasionally dragging the ball left a second time, and go around on that side instead of carrying out the drag right.

TOSS AND GO

This is a means by which you can move quickly with the ball and eliminate your opponent simultaneously. If the defender is square in his stance (see figure 6.3) and your vision and timing are right, you can toss the ball through your opponent's legs or behind him and accelerate, which means that your opponent needs to turn quickly and chase.

The toss and go is a simple technique that punishes defenders who are out of position or 'square' in their stance, but be careful not to throw the ball too far behind your opponent into the territory of another opponent. This skill requires very little fancy stick work but can be just as effective and even more reliable than a drag, because there are fewer variables that can go wrong within the execution of the skill. Also, you can maintain better vision off the ball as you approach the defender because the skill requires fewer contacts between the stick and ball. The ball handler gives up tight possession momentarily, so be sure that there is space ahead for the ball and the ball handler to move into.

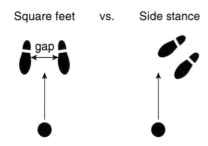

Figure 6.3 Toss and go.

THE JINK

This is a skill used to get past the lunging stick of your opponent when his stick is flat or very low to the ground. The jink is the means by which you lift the ball very slightly, or 'jink' it, over the opposition player's stick as he tries to make a tackle. You can develop this skill on both sides of your body.

   The jink is a skill you can bring into your game to evade tacklers even if you are not very strong. It's usually a matter of simply sliding your stick under the ball as you run using the momentum of the ball. The more you practice this skill, the more comfortable you will feel about trying it in a game situation. (See figure 6.4.)

Figure 6.4 Gently slide your stick under the ball using its forward momentum to lift it over the stick of the defender. Lift it a couple of inches off the ground to evade a lunging stick, but be careful not to lift it too high so that the umpire considers it to be dangerous.

36   DOUBLE-HAND JINK

Purpose

To understand the principle of the jink and to become comfortable executing it in a mobile situation.

Procedure

In the beginning, practice jinking the ball a couple of inches off the ground as you walk, then jog with the ball on your forestick. Slide your stick under the ball as you move forward, and gently lift the ball a couple of inches into the air. As you become more comfortable with the technique, place small obstacles in your way (sticks, stick bags, clothing), and gently lift the ball over the top. Be careful not to lift the ball too high in the air because you run the risk of being penalised by the umpire for bringing about dangerous play, particularly when entering the attacking circle or in the defensive circle. The skill is in applying a deft lift of only a very small distance off the ground.

37   REVERSE-STICK JINK

Purpose
To develop the ability to jink the ball on your reverse-stick side with only one hand.

Procedure
When you can jink proficiently with two hands on your stick (on both the left and the right side of your body), practice executing the same skill with only your left hand on your reverse-stick side so that you can use this skill wide to the left of your body to increase your repertoire. This is not easy to do, but surprisingly it does not necessarily require brute strength. To begin, have your left hand lower on the stick for added strength.

THE 2-ON-1

This is a principle of elimination that is useful all over the field and over any distance within the confines of the field. The 2-on-1 allows you to isolate and punish opponents, and its implementation can become a game within the game, or a mini-battle if you like!

The 2-on-1 situation means that two team-mates, one in possession of the ball, can pass around one opponent to eliminate that player from the contest. On the other hand, one attacker can use the other player as a decoy and simply sell a dummy as though to pass in that direction before continuing forward with the ball without making a pass. Either way, this is a two-against-one situation which does not require complicated (and high risk) stick work.

The 2-on-1 can be a simple way of eliminating an opponent, but it is generally underused, perhaps because it doesn't look flashy enough! You can create mini-2-on-1s all over the field, and if you recognise the appropriate time to do it, your execution is slick and your timing is right, you should get past almost every time. In small-game situations in training or in real match situations, you can look to set up the play to isolate your opponent in this way.

Here are some basic tips for the 2-on-1. The player with the ball draws or commits the defender. When the defender is drawn towards the ball carrier, the ball is passed as early as possible to a team-mate who is typically running in a position just behind the ball carrier (backwards of square).

KEY NOTE
You should never underestimate the influence you can have on an opponent's movement by selling a convincing dummy using only your body weight or small movements of your stick.

The variation on this theme is the one-time wall pass. When you have made the initial pass in a 2-on-1 situation, be ready to receive the ball back immediately with a bunt pass from your team-mate. Your defender will likely turn to the player to whom you have passed the ball initially and be ill-prepared to intercept the pass back to you. (See figure 6.5a.) You can also make a sharp lead past your opponent and receive the ball in a higher position, which eliminates the defender. (See figure 6.5b.) Of course, if the defender does not go to the player to whom you passed the ball, he can continue moving into space uncontested. As always, watch the defender and make your play accordingly.

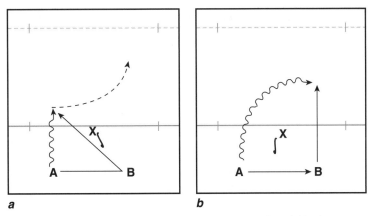

Figure 6.5 (*a*) Be ready to receive the ball back quickly from your team-mate. (*b*) Lead past the defender so that you are available to receive the ball back in better offensive position.

Another option you have in a 2-on-1 situation is to dummy as though to pass to your team-mate who does not end up receiving the ball, just as you would when executing the first movement of the drags as outlined earlier in the chapter. This second player is an important part of the equation because she creates a passing option and therefore puts the defender in two minds as to what the ball carrier will do next. When it is clear that the defender has committed his weight to intercepting your pass (left or right), move the ball back into a position of strength and accelerate into space to eliminate your opponent without passing the ball. You can physically fake a pass (move your stick over the ball) to commit the defender to that end. When he is committed to intercepting the fake pass, accelerate forward into space without making a pass. (See figure 6.6.)

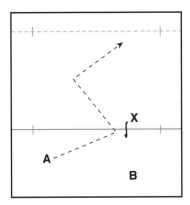

Figure 6.6 If the defender moves to anticipate the pass, accelerate forward without passing the ball.

38   2-ON-1

Purpose

To practice using the 2-on-1. This can become a 3-on-2 or a 4-on-3 and so on.

Procedure

Mark a confined area and a goal area on the endline. The two players with the ball try to get past a solitary defender and dribble the ball over the endline to score.

39   2-ON-1 SHOOT, PASS, MOVE

Purpose

To increase the relevance of the 2-on-1 skill to a match situation.

Procedure

Introduce another skill such as a pass, goal shot or direction change for the ball carrier once the defender is eliminated. To make this most effective, remember to cut in behind the defender. The defender turns to chase, and the player with the ball then tries to shoot at goal, make a pass or move sharply in another direction to cut the line of the defender.

Elimination skills and the appropriate use of them are difficult to get right, so be patient. Start slowly in a passive situation, and gradually increase the speed at which you attempt the skills using an appropriately passive or competitive defender, depending upon the level of competitiveness that you want. Value the various and simple 2-on-1 elimination techniques. To completely eliminate the defender and to get the best result for your skill execution, remember to cut in behind the defender by changing the line of your movement with the ball. Learn to move comfortably to your left and right, and pay particular attention to the side that you don't favour naturally. Your ability to move in both directions will keep your opponents guessing, which will make life easier for you!

Remember that the really good players minimise the ball movement from side to side (that is, they keep movement simple), which minimises the chance of error. There will be times when lateral movement using the drags is necessary, so in these instances try to keep your stick on the ball as much as you can, and use your body movement to sell the dummy while carrying the ball in passing position.

CHAPTER 7

GOAL SHOOTING

All the skills you have developed for use in general play are also useful in the goal circle. In particular, the short, sharp leading skills create opportunities for you to get the ball, solid trapping skills allow you to control the ball in a good position to make an effective goal shot and slight variations on the passing methods that you use in general play are also used for goal shooting. There are many aspects to consider when shooting at goal, including penetrating the circle in the best possible position to give yourself the best chance to score, placement (often more useful than powerful shots), and precise skill execution and smart shot selection are paramount.

PENETRATING THE CIRCLE

The smart teams create circle penetrations that give them options to move and shoot either way once they are inside the circle. Entering the circle in the best possible position means that you can make goal shots that have a good angle to the goal and therefore the best chance of scoring, or they give your team-mates the chance for a second or third chance to score via a rebound.

Your team should set up the play so as to enter through the middle of the circle as much as possible and away from the baseline or endline in particular. Obviously at times this wide-circle entry is necessary, but defenders try to channel you there for a reason: It limits your passing options and gives you a smaller shooting angle, and the risk to the defending team is therefore minimised.

I remember talking to the coach of the Dutch team one evening after a match. He said he didn't particularly rate a forward who had played in the match because even though she had clever skills, defenders could easily minimise her impact by channelling her wide of the centre of the goal. I'm sure the defenders on your team try to do the same thing to their opposing forwards. Ask the defenders on your team how they go about channelling forwards wide and what they would like (or not like) the forwards to do in response. You can also learn from your team-mates by assuming their roles (defenders become forwards and vice versa) during training sessions.

If you do need to enter the circle deep on the backline or endline, and you find yourself running with the ball along that line, try to make a pass back into the middle of the

KEY NOTE
It is the quality of the attacking moves you make, not the number generated that is significant during a game.

circle (generally aim for the penalty spot) to a player who is on a better shooting angle. If there is no obvious pass to a central player, try to commit the goalkeeper to you with the possibility of a low-percentage shot on goal, and then pass across the face of the goal (eliminating the goalkeeper) or on a sharper angle back to the penalty spot for an opportunistic forward to shoot at goal.

40   BASELINE RUNNING AND PASSING

Purpose

To practice entering the circle in a contested manner on the baseline, committing the goalkeeper to a baseline shot on goal and passing back to the penalty spot or the top of the circle to a player who is in better position to shoot in a contested situation. This is a good opportunity for the goalkeeper to practice decision making in a fluid situation. It's also useful leading and shooting practice for the forwards.

Procedure

Set up with an attacker and a defender on the penalty spot and the circle top. Play a 1-on-1 (or a 2-on-1) into the circle through the cones from a wide position. Once the attacker is through that play, she runs along the baseline and passes to one of the other two attackers in a contested situation. That player shoots at goal, or the defender who tackles or makes an interception makes a pass to an outlet target. If the goalkeeper tries to read that play and leaves a gap, the baseline player can shoot at goal. (See figure 7.1.)

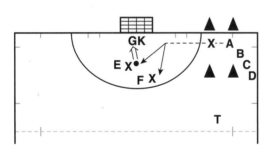

Figure 7.1   Baseline running and passing.

The total number of circle penetrations can be an indicative statistic for post game analysis, but the quality of the penetrations is more critical. There is no point entering the circle 30 times in a game if you are not in good position to create a shot on goal or another attacking opportunity such as a penalty corner. It's better to have half the penetrations and generate a higher percentage of good goal-shooting opportunities from those circle entries.

The closer to the centre of the field you are when you enter the circle, the greater the choice of shots on goal (and passes) available to you when you get inside the scoring area. The better the shooting angle (the more central your shooting position), the more difficult it will be for the goalkeeper to make a save, and the better your chance of getting a good result for your shot on goal. Also, in this centralised position, you can pass either way, and your team-mate will still be in position to have a good shooting angle and choice of goal-shooting techniques once he has received the ball. (See figure 7.2.) Given the fluid nature of the game, these rules apply to anyone (not just the strikers) who finds himself in an offensive position as your team works towards creating attacking plays and shots on goal.

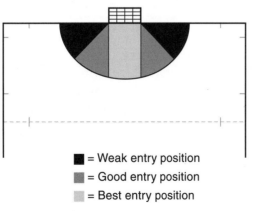

■ = Weak entry position

■ = Good entry position

■ = Best entry position

Figure 7.2   Circle penetration.

Guidelines for High Forwards

Before we get into the detail of goal shooting, take a look at some of the rules for strikers that our squad developed in preparation for the Olympic Games:

- Assume your defensive role when the opposition has the ball, and remember that everyone has a role in defence, not just the defenders.
- Score when you have the chance and 'kick, bite and scratch' to do so!
- Win penalty corners when appropriate and when you cannot get a good shot away or make a pass to a player in a better position.
- If you turn the ball over, recover quickly and pay particular attention to the first 10 yards of your recovery. This can be the difference between putting the pressure back on the player with the ball and letting him get away.
- Create outlet options by leading back into the play when necessary.
- Get in behind the defenders and beat your opponent in the attacking half when you have the opportunity.
- Try to receive the ball behind your defender so that you don't need to eliminate him when you have the ball in your possession. Make the play easy for yourself!
- Make sure your basic skills, including the trap, are well rehearsed and second nature, but don't take these skills for granted. Practice in pressurised situations.
- Make sure your positioning is as useful as possible to your team. For example, one striker might be high up the field to create depth for the attack, but all players should be in contact (verbal and visual) with each other so that your relative positioning is organized.

In the circle, you should

- get low with your stick near the ground;
- always be alert;
- make short, sharp leads;
- be ready to make deflections; and
- have strength in your positioning and when you have the ball.

USING PLACEMENT VERSUS POWER

A common error that players make in the attacking circle is to think that they need to get the ball moving as hard as possible towards the goal. Power is useful in many instances, but placement of the ball in a particular part of the goal is *always* critical. The speed with which you get the shot away (as opposed to the speed of the ball) is also important. A powerful shot wide of the goal might earn a gasp from the crowd, but it won't require a save from the goalkeeper, and so it won't earn your fellow forwards a second chance at a shot on goal through a rebound or a tip in after a sloppy save from the goalkeeper.

Remember also that although the goal circle is a busy and congested area, sometimes you have more time than you think to prepare. In many instances you can make certain of the quality of the shot on goal rather than rushing your shot execution and hoping for

KEY NOTE
Goal shooting is all about making the most of your chances. Be an opportunist!

the best. Get the goal shot away quickly if you need to, but take time if you have it to get your technique right. In this way you give yourself the best possible chance of scoring. If you get the ball moving towards goal, anything can happen. A shot on target (regardless of its power) means that the goalkeeper will need to make a save. That can bring about a costly defensive error and create a rebound opportunity if not a goal.

Shoot the Pro Side

'Shoot the pro side' was a motto our team used over the years, and the Hockey-roos still use it today. The 'pro side' is the side of the goal opposite to the goal shooter's position. For example, if you are shooting from wide on the right of the circle, you should generally aim for the opposite post (the left post as the striker looks at it), unless there is a large and obvious space on the near side between the goalkeeper and the goalpost.

Shooting the pro side creates several new opportunities for the attacking team, but a goal shot fired at the near post provides little opportunity for a deflection or a second chance for your team-mates. If the shot goes wide on the non-pro side, the ball will simply crash out of play into the side of the goal and provide no rebound or deflection possibilities for the attacking players in the circle. Similarly, if the goalkeeper gets a touch on the ball, it will be with the outside leg or hand, and the ball will very easily be knocked out of play without penalty—a perfect result for the defensive team!

The following are the benefits of shooting the pro side:

- If the goalkeeper gets a touch on the ball, it is likely to rebound back into the circle. If this occurs it may fall to an attacker directly or into a position in which an attacker can recover the play and create another scoring opportunity.

- If a shot goes wide of the goal, another attacker waiting on, or diving to, the far post can tip it in.

- A diving attacker can make a deflection from inside the circle, which is very hard for the goalkeeper to save because this will happen at high speed.

In goal-shooting drills you can penalise players for not shooting to the pro side by assigning push-ups or lap running or whatever motivates them to take care to apply this principle. When appropriate, you can eliminate players from the drill until the last shooter is standing.

Second- and third-chance attacking scenarios are less common if the shot is to the non-pro side. It is also easier for defenders, including the goalkeeper, to knock the ball out of play and away from immediate danger on the non-pro side.

MAKING THE GOAL SHOT

The best goal scorers are rarely the biggest and strongest players on a team. Rather they are cunning and alert players who anticipate well. They have a strong awareness of where the goal is in relation to their position and that of the ball. Very good goal scorers are rare, so if you can develop your skills in this area, it is likely to set you apart from other forwards who are vying with you for selection in the team.

In the circle, keep your knees bent and your weight forward (be on your toes, not flat-footed) and particularly if you are close to the goalmouth, try to get your left hand (at the top of the handle of the stick) to touch the ground so that your stick remains low and potentially closer to the approaching ball. If you are low to the ground, you will minimise the distance you need to move your stick in reaction to late deflections or a firm pass from close range. You will also be in the best position to react to the eventualities in the circle. By anticipating where the ball is likely to rebound, you can be ready for that critical scoring opportunity, which could change the result of the game. (See figure 7.3.)

Steve 'China' Davies is one of the best goal scorers to have played the game of hockey. Once described as the Maradona of hockey, he played 274 games for Australia and scored 140 international goals. He played in three Olympic Games for two bronze medals and a silver, three World Cup tournaments and nine Champions Trophy tournaments. Now he is heavily involved in the sport as a coaching consultant in Australia and around the world, so he knows what he is talking about when it comes to goal shooting! These are his tips:

- **Attitude.** As a striker you must be very determined to score the goal and have a desire to get your name on the scoring list or in the paper—whatever motivates you! You need to be cunning and try to outsmart defenders, which is a natural feature of top-class strikers. You need to have a degree of selfishness about your game in order to take risks at the appropriate time. A very good striker is one who can make the correct decision about when to shoot and when to find a better option in the circle.

- **Skills.** Good trapping skills under pressure are critical. If you can't make good traps, you won't create opportunities for scoring, so stay low and alert. Be aware of what is going on around you by knowing where the defenders and your support players are around you, and have a good feel for where you are in relation to the goal. The ability to read the play

Figure 7.3 Get low, keep your weight on your toes and be ready!

'Eighty percent of field goals are scored 10 metres from the net or closer, so be very alert for opportunities in this area.'—Steve Davies

Figure 7.4 A shorter grip on the stick will mean a quicker shot on goal. Drop your left hand to meet your right hand for this shot, and use your wrists.

(anticipate the play before it happens) or second-guess what defenders and team-mates will do next will give you an edge. A striker needs to have a variety of shots and excellent shot selection and decision making to back it up. So practise the shots you are not good at. Fast hand and foot speed is essential for making quality shots in minimal time.

- **Hitting.** If you are hitting the ball at goal, you can rarely afford the time to take a big backswing. The time taken to do this allows the defenders an opportunity to steal the ball from under your nose, because you're not protecting the ball by keeping your stick close to it. You can shorten your backswing by bringing your left hand down the stick to meet your right hand (see figure 7.4). This may not be natural for you, but with practice you can master this to great effect. With a shorter backswing, the shot becomes a wristier hit than you might otherwise use in general play. But it's effective because it's quick and more deceptive than a hit with a loopier, slower backswing.

- **Placement.** Good goal shooting is always about accuracy and excellent placement of the ball. Even if you hit the ball as hard as you can, it won't be an effective shot unless it is on target. This means that it at least requires a save for the goalkeeper, provides a 'tip-in' (a slight touch) opportunity for your fellow forwards or provides a chance for a rebound. Sometimes players sacrifice accuracy and placement for power, but this is not necessarily the best compromise for the team. The opposite of this (sacrificing power for accuracy) is usually more useful.

Footwork

As is the case with all the skills of the game, good footwork can make the difference between executing a skill with precision and wasting a good opportunity. Footwork is the component that players tend to neglect when they are rushing, tired or under pressure. Get this important component right, and you will be in good position to execute your shot on goal with maximum precision and strength.

When you have made the trap, keep your stick on the ball while you get your feet into the best possible position. This involves being balanced with your feet lined up with your target in the same way that they would be for a pass (see figure 7.5). Although this is the ideal footwork when you are hitting the ball, you may need to compromise on this ideal position if you are rushed. On the other hand, you may choose not to hit the ball and select another shooting option because there is insufficient time to get your feet into good position. You may also make a pass or win a penalty corner instead of shooting.

If you keep your stick on the ball as you get your feet into position, you will protect the ball from the opposition while you get your footwork right. Once your feet are lined up in

Figure 7.5 Stick in the horizontal position.

the direction of your target (as for a pass in general play), you are ready to make the shot. This ideal positioning (your feet in line with your target) remains the same whether you choose to hit or push the ball, but you will not always have time to get this positioning perfect, especially in the attacking circle.

Another common error for forwards is to rush the goal shot and, in so doing, disregard the position of the feet. This unbalanced situation is sometimes necessary, but you will get better value for your shot on goal if you take all the time available to you to get your footwork right.

Rebounding

Forwards tend to relax after making the shot on goal and when they are not directly involved in the play. Shot execution is only one component of your work in the circle, and more often than not you will be one of the players 'off' the ball, either watching and admiring the good work of a team-mate or more appropriately waiting for and expecting a rebound opportunity to come to you. This off-the-ball role is very important, and it is simple to improve your skill in this area to increase your attacking potency. Anyone can learn to do it if they put their mind to it because it is a matter of attitude rather than a complex physical skill, but not everyone places a high value on this.

If you don't have the ball, wish it to come to you and remain alert with your weight on the balls of your feet. Keep your knees bent and your stick low to the ground. If you can do these things, you will be in good position to react to the situation in the attacking circle. This is a very congested area, and there are many opportunities for a quick change in circumstances and fortune. You just need to be ready to take your chance. It takes only a small deflection for the ball to change its line of movement and fall to your advantage when, only moments earlier, it seemed as though the outcome would be completely different.

If you are the player who has made the shot, keep your momentum moving forward in the follow-through and expect a rebound. Don't admire your handiwork and forget your next role! The ball probably won't come back to you directly, but if it does, you need to be ready for it.

41   SHOOTING WITH REBOUND BOARDS

Purpose

To introduce and practice rebounding skills with the initial shot coming from different angles.

Procedure

Using wooden boards or a mini-trampoline, set these up just wide of the goal (angled slightly so that the ball rebounds into the circle) and have another player hit at it from varying angles. The player practicing the rebound controls the rebounding ball and shoots at goal. You can have three or four players waiting for the rebound—each of them must be ready every time. To understand the different rebounding angles, vary the angle of the initial hit and that of the rebound boards. Vary the distance and speed of the initial shot to manipulate the necessary reaction time.

42   REBOUNDING IN SHOOTING DRILLS

Purpose

To make rebounding instinctive in a live situation.

Procedure

In all goal-shooting drills, make sure that you have spare players ready and waiting in the circle for rebound opportunities. Play the drills out until the ball leaves the circle. You can have a spare player or a coach on the backline to throw extra balls into the circle if the initial shot does not rebound back into play.

43   REBOUNDING OR DEFLECTING

Purpose

For rebounding practice, two players (A and B) at the 25-yard line pass between each other in a confined area as they move towards the circle. One of these players shoots as soon as he crosses into the circle. Meanwhile, two players (C and D) begin on the cones on either side of the passing players and sprint to the baseline or around a cone and back into the circle to pick up the rebound. (See figure 7.6.)

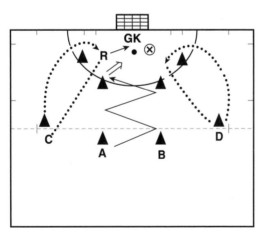

Figure 7.6   Rebounding or deflecting.

Variation

To practice deflecting, players C and D cut straight into the circle (instead of heading to the baseline to make a deflection), which requires the shooting player to shoot according to the position of the deflecting player. Change the entry point into the circle to introduce different angles of the rebounds and deflections. You can mix the two variations into one drill also.

Shooting Options

The flick, push and reverse flick are not powerful options, but they can be effective in the attacking circle in the right situation. These shots can get the ball moving towards the goal, and the worst-case scenario for the attacking team is that they require the goalkeeper to make a save that creates another rebound opportunity.

Even many years after her retirement, Jackie Pereira, who played 179 games and scored 109 goals for the Australian women's hockey team, is still considered one of the best goal scorers of all time. Jackie was one of the more diminutive players in the game, but she was clever about the way she approached her goal shooting.

Ever an opportunist, Jackie was always ready to pounce on defensive errors, and she rarely hit the ball to score her goals. She usually placed the ball cleverly with a push when the goalkeeper was unprepared, off balance or off her line. There is a very small window of opportunity to do this, but Jackie had the knack. Also, she was prepared to dive in the goal circle and make opportunities happen where most players considered that none existed.

Push and Flick

For a push at goal, you will be in the same low body position with your stick on the ball at all times as we have discussed in chapter 2. There is no backswing, so it is a quick shot to execute, but there is less power than for some of the other shooting alternatives such as the hit. Because this shot is quick, you can punish the goalkeeper when he is off balance by firing the ball without notice past the foot that is supporting the body weight of the goalkeeper because that will be the one that is slowest to move.

When you shoot at goal, you can raise the ball as long as it is not dangerous. To execute the flick (as you would in general play), angle your stick slightly backwards, get your stick underneath the ball and follow through to your target. (See figure 7.7a-d.) Ultimately, you should be able to generate the same power for a flick as you do for a push at goal. You can also disguise the flick as a flat push. This is much the same as executing a push shot, but you add elevation with a slight change in your technique at the last minute so as to get underneath the ball by angling your stick slightly backwards.

Reverse Flick

This is a difficult shot to execute with power, but you can work on getting that result with practice. With the ball on the left side of your body, turn your body to face the ball. With your head over the ball and your hands apart (left hand at the top and right hand lower down), follow through towards your target. The momentum of your shot may mean that you end up with all your weight on your right foot and with your left foot in the air. Begin by starting with your stick on the ball; as you improve your skill, try to approach the shot from a distance so that you step into the ball.

The principle is the same for flicking on your forestick side, except that for the flick on the reverse, the ball will be closer to your body so that you can get your head over the ball and your weight behind it. Your body will be further from the ball for the basic push on the forestick side.

Figure 7.7 Flick at the goal: (*a*) Angle your stick backwards slightly, (*b*) get your stick under the ball, (*c*) and (*d*) follow through towards your target.

44 TARGETING THE FLICK, LOB REVERSE FLICK AND PUSH AT GOAL

Purpose

To increase the level of shooting specificity with power.

Procedure

Receive the ball in the circle (vary the position) from a team-mate, and flick or push the ball into the net. Place targets in the corners and keep your score. (Car tyres are useful as targets; you can tie them to the top corners and place them in the bottom corners of the net.) Rotate through the shooting targets so that you do sets of four, aiming to hit one in each corner in each set.

45 REVERSE FLICK

Purpose

To get the technique for the reverse flick in order so that you are comfortable to execute this skill in a game situation.

Procedure

Line up 10 balls about 2 or 3 metres (6 or 9 feet) out from goal. One by one, flick the balls into the net as quickly as possible because you will usually be rushed if you are choosing this shot in a game situation. Vary the distance from the goal for each set. Our coaches made a fake goalkeeper out of a wooden plank and dressed it in goal keeping gear for practicing rebounding and executing raised shots at goal, but you can use any obstacle you like to practice the reverse flick over a goalkeeper in order to make the shooting skill more realistic. (See figure 7.8.)

Figure 7.8 Reverse flick.

Scoop or Lob

If you simply want to raise the ball over the goalkeeper on your reverse side, you need elevation more than power. With the ball in the same position as just described (or immediately in front of you), get your head over the ball once again, but dip your left hand so that the handle of the stick drops as you get your stick under the ball to achieve elevation. Using your right hand, which is lower down the stick, lift the ball at goal as though you are 'scooping' or lobbing the ball into the air.

You can use this scoop to clear the goalkeeper who has moved out of the net and towards the top of the circle by 'lobbing' the ball over the top as she approaches. This is a difficult skill to execute, but if it works, you will eliminate the goalkeeper and have a good chance to score. (See figure 7.9.)

Figure 7.9 Dip your left hand and scoop with your right to achieve elevation.

46   SCOOPING OR LOBBING

Purpose

To practice the lob or scoop from the top of the circle. This shot can beat an approaching goalkeeper.

Procedure

In a stationary position at first, line the balls up just inside the top of the circle. Lob the ball at goal (using an obstacle to lift the ball over if you like). As you get better, move with the ball into the circle and scoop the ball at goal as though to lob it over the approaching goalkeeper. Introduce an approaching goalkeeper to make the skill more realistic.

Chip Shot and Undercut

This chip shot on goal is a raised hit at goal, usually achieved with a short backswing. Angle the face of your stick backwards according to the desired elevation of the shot. The goalkeeper may be moving towards you at the top of the circle; as he slides to tackle or block, or the moment you sense that the goalkeeper's weight is committed to dropping to the ground, chip the ball over the top of that player. This doesn't need to be a powerful shot; the ball simply needs enough elevation to clear the charging goalkeeper.

The undercut is a similar shot on goal to the chip shot. It is raised as it moves towards goal but is more powerful than the chip shot. Hit the ball with all your might, but angle your stick slightly (more if you want increased elevation), depending on the elevation you are looking for, just as for the chip shot. Remember, if the ball misses the target and goes over or past the net (this happens often with this shot because it is difficult to execute with both power and control), there will be no second or third opportunities to shoot in that particular play. If you are going to elevate the shot, you may be well served to aim your shot higher than hand height (hand height is a relatively easy save for the goalkeeper) and aim for the top corners of the goal, but there is obviously a greater margin for error here because this is a more difficult shot and the target is smaller. If you miss your target, you will miss the goal entirely! (See figure 7.10.)

KEY NOTE
One of the easiest shots for a goalkeeper to save is a shot at hand height, so often it's better to keep the ball low to the ground. The lower shot requires the goalkeeper to use a more difficult foot save. In all that protective leg gear, hands move faster than feet!

Figure 7.10 Angle your stick backwards slightly to achieve elevation and hit through the ball.

Squeeze Shot

This is a difficult shot to get right, but if you can master it, you will bring another deceptive and raised shot into your repertoire. The squeeze shot is executed with the downward action of your stick towards the ball. The ball is positioned slightly behind your back foot. The downward action of your stick will 'squeeze' the ball into the ground to force it into the air. Your swing will be from above and slightly behind the ball, with your stick making contact with the upper back of the ball.

47   MOVE AND SQUEEZE

Purpose

To become comfortable with the squeezing technique.

Procedure

Practice moving (walk, then jog) on the field by gently squeezing the ball slightly in the air. As you get the feel for it, practice increasing the intensity of the squeeze so that you are eventually shooting at goal and achieving power as well as accuracy.

This shot is relatively quick to execute with only a short backswing required. It will surprise your opponents because of the speed with which you can execute it. Also, it will look like a regular hit for much of the preparation. (See figure 7.11.)

Figure 7.11 Use a downward action and make contact with the upper back of the ball to squeeze it into the ground to force it into the air. You can see the spray of water as the downward action of the stick forces the ball into the air.

Deflecting

This is a useful goal-scoring alternative for forwards. With the ball travelling at great speed from any distance inside or outside the circle, a good deflection is very difficult for a goalkeeper to stop. With a slight touch, the deflection changes the line of the ball (the direction in which the ball is moving) at the last moment, which makes it a difficult shot for the goalkeeper to react to and stop. There is no backswing required, and this shot is very subtle and well disguised.

Don't be tempted to swing across the line of the ball as it approaches. Rather, anticipate the line early, place your stick in the line of the ball and by angling your stick appropriately, wait for the ball to arrive and strike your stick. Try not to have a backswing and 'hit' the ball, because this will only make the timing of the skill all the more difficult. Let the pace of the ball do the work for you. Use a ball machine to fire balls repetitively from the same angle to get your positioning right.

When you have practiced deflecting the ball for some time, you will get a feeling for the best angles on which to execute the skill, relative to the player who is delivering the ball. This is the hard part. In most instances you will need to be roughly on the ball side of the centre of the goal, or between the near goalpost (to the passing player) and the player making the pass if you are to make a successful deflection at goal when the ball is passed from a wide position.

Don't swing at the ball because this significantly increases the degree of difficulty and the margin for error. Allow the ball to strike your stick rather than making your stick strike at the ball. If you are too far from where the ball has travelled (usually too close to the far post from where the ball began its journey or too far on the other side of centre from the pass), the deflection will probably go wide of the net. Aim to be no wider or further away from the pass than a central circle position when the ball is hit at you for a deflection. As a rule of thumb, if you are not central, then be on the pass side of the central penalty spot position rather than the non-pass side. The earlier you make contact with the ball before it reaches the centre of the goal, the better the shooting angle you will have. The available net space will be larger.

Your positioning in the circle will depend largely on the position from which the ball is delivered. At training when you are learning to deflect the ball, do so from wherever your instinct takes you. After each attempted deflection, measure (roughly) the distance by which you have missed the net and move that distance in the other direction the next time the ball comes at you from the same position. If you are hitting your target, then no adjustment is required.

Trial and error is the only way to gain a good understanding of the best positioning for deflecting, and you need to learn to readjust your body positioning and the angle of your stick according to the pass, ball speed and the passing angle. Eventually, you will get a good feel for your positioning in the circle and you will get there without thinking much about it. An example of being closer than the centre of the goal is illustrated in figure 7.12.

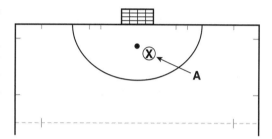

Figure 7.12 Use the centre of the circle as a guide (the penalty spot) and try to be on the nearer side of the centre of goal to the passing player rather than the far side.

48   SHOOT, LEAD, DEFLECT AND REBOUND

Purpose

To improve the deflecting techniques in live play. This drill also combines well with general shooting, leading, diving and rebounding practice and requires that the deflecting player be ready for the second play after the initial shot on goal.

Procedure

The balls are to the left and right of the attacking circle, and the deflecting players are lined up outside the circle in a central position. Player A on the left makes a pass to player B at the top of the circle. Player B shoots at goal, then leads into the circle to deflect a pass from player C outside the right side of the circle. An attacking player also sits close to each post (players D and E) for a rebound to dive at the post or tip the ball in if it goes wide of the net. To practice deflecting and rebounding from both sides of the circle, alternate sides and angle of the first pass, and alternate shooting positions as you go. (See figure 7.13.)

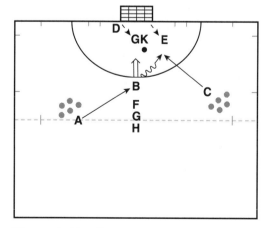

Figure 7.13 Shoot, lead, deflect and rebound.

Low Reverse Shot

Nikki Hudson, one of the most formidable strikers in the women's game and certainly one of the Hockeyroos' star strikers, is very good at shooting with a hit at goal on her reverse side.

Advantages of reverse-stick shooting include:

- It adds another shot to your repertoire and allows you to turn both ways to get a quick shot away, increasing the options available to you.
- Your ability to do so keeps the defender guessing as to which way you will turn, making it very difficult for the defender to close your shot down.
- You can protect the ball with your body as you make the shot.
- It is difficult for the goalkeeper to read where the ball is going because most of the time the shooter does not know where it is going either!

Nikki describes some disadvantages of reverse-stick shooting:

- You don't necessarily have time to position yourself perfectly to make the shot, so the difficulty associated with placing your feet in relation to the ball increases the possibility for error.

'It is about getting the correct technique right. If you have that, it doesn't matter how hard you hit it because it will be on target and will at least create opportunities such as rebounds for other players. Your footwork and sharp preparation are really important because a split second can mean the difference between scoring and not scoring.'—Nikki Hudson

- This is a difficult shot to get right, so you must concentrate on the technique.
- If you don't pay full attention to your skill execution and get the ball into the best possible position, you will find yourself reaching for the ball (reducing the power you can achieve), or you might lift it. If the ball is too close to your body, you are likely to hook it wide of the goal.

These are Nikki's coaching points:

- Turn your stick so that the round side faces the ground and the hook of the stick is pointing towards the target.
- Position your right foot just behind the line of the ball about three-quarters of a stick length away from the ball.
- Bend your knees and get low to make clean contact with the ball.
- Position your hands together in a comfortable position (about halfway down the stick to allow for a quicker and more controlled shot).
- Keep your backswing as low to the ground as possible.
- Keep your stick low to the ground as it moves towards the ball. Swing on a gradual angle if you can't slide your stick along the ground for the duration of the swing. Avoid moving your stick on a sharp angle down towards the ball, which is a common mistake when preparation time is limited.
- Aim to make contact with the ball about 7 to 10 centimetres (3 to 4 inches) down from the hook of the stick.
- Keep your head down on impact with the ball, and follow through so that your weight is on your right leg. If you lean backwards as you make contact, you will sacrifice power and accuracy because you will slice across the face of the ball.
- At the moment of impact, imagine a line running through your shoulders and towards the target. If your alignment (the line from your shoulders to your target) is correct, your hit should be on target, as is the case for hitting and pushing on the forestick side.
- Try to get your right leg approximately parallel with the ground. With your target to your right, your hips face forward (towards the ball) and your upper body ultimately rotates towards the goal with the follow-through. (See figure 7.14 a-c.)
- When shooting from an angle, aim for the far post to allow a team-mate the chance for a deflection if your shot misses the goal (the pro side, as discussed earlier).
- Practice executing the same technique every time. If this is not possible, limit the extent to which the technique varies on each occasion.
- Don't feel as though you have to hit the ball really hard. If you hit it with a reasonable amount of power and with the correct technique, the shot will be on target and will surprise the goalkeeper sufficiently to make up for the lack of power. This is a more difficult shot to read than a hit on the flat-stick side.

A final word of caution: Repetition shooting for an untrained player does result in a very sore butt!

Figure 7.14 (*a*) Bend your knees, have your hands together and get low to make clean contact with the ball. (*b*) Keep your backswing and follow-through as low to the ground as possible and try to get your upper right leg approximately parallel with the ground. (*c*) Your target is to your right with your hips facing towards the ball as you make contact with the ball.

49   REVERSE-HIT REPETITION

Purpose

To help you become comfortable with the reverse-hit technique.

Procedure

Initially, practice in a stationary position close to the goal. Slowly begin hitting the ball in this way, making sure that the ball stays on the ground. You may need to begin in a kneeling position on your left knee. Gradually learn to step into the ball and increase the power of the shot and the distance from the goal.

50   RECEIVE AND HIT ON REVERSE

Purpose

To become comfortable receiving the ball from any direction and controlling it in position to execute the reverse hit.

Procedure

Practice receiving the ball on both sides from a team-mate, but each time make the trap so that you are in position to hit the ball on your reverse. As you practice, you will become increasingly aware of the best position in which to control the ball to execute the reverse hit.

Diving for the Ball

This is one skill that I believe is undervalued as a good scoring opportunity by most for- wards, particularly women. Diving goals are not only exciting for the crowd, but they also win games by creating something out of what seems to be nothing. Diving is a last resort because obviously you are better placed to execute a shot on goal if you are on your feet. But if all other possibilities are lost, diving at the ball is a useful addition to your attacking armoury. A diving forward is difficult for the defenders to mark, and often this action is unexpected.

When you dive, you can trap or deflect the balls that would otherwise be out of your reach and fall to the benefit of your opponent. You can also get to the balls that would otherwise go out of play altogether. By diving, sometimes you can make a deflection at the last minute, which will change the line of the ball and give the goalkeeper very little time to react.

Try to make sure that there is an attacker waiting on each goalpost. If no one from your team is there, try to get there yourself if it is appropriate. We used to describe this 'getting to the post' (including diving to the post) mentality as making the goal wider, because if you arrive at the post or dive to the post as another player has a shot on goal, a wide shot can be trapped or deflected into the net instead of ending up out of play on both sides of the net.

Diving in the circle can create something from nothing. Rarely is there a price for diving in the circle if all other shooting alternatives have been ruled out. The goalkeeper can only be concerned with the immediate goal shot, and a diving forward will prob- ably be unmarked at the crucial moment. That player can get a valuable touch on a ball that has been left by the goalkeeper because it is going wide of the goal. You will keep the goalkeeper guessing and potentially distract him and the other defenders from their primary tasks such as making basic positions and traps. He will probably not expect this extra scoring possibility either, and this might be enough for you to create an opportunity where there seemed to be none.

Diving is not a difficult trick. Simply, it is about getting into a potential goal scoring position every time there is an opportunity. Expect that the ball will make it through the traffic in the circle, and get there in case it does. Most often you will pick yourself up off the ground without having made contact with the ball, but you will eventually be rewarded with an invaluable touch on a ball that has been passed across the face of goal or has been shot wide of goal.

51   DIVING FOR THE BALL

Purpose

To become comfortable with the diving technique.

Procedure

For this drill to be safe, the field must be very wet so that you can slide. You can use a wet plastic sheet for increased safety. As a player passes from the right of the circle across the face of goal and in front of the player practicing the skill, dive with your stick in your left hand. Don't just drop to the ground, but run forward and dive so that you slide along the ground rather than land with a thump. This will make diving a less painful experience! More important, practice in game situations because it has more to do with your attitude, anticipation and awareness of the right time to dive than the physical skill itself.

Watching the Goalkeeper

Here are a few tips to remember when shooting on goal.

- **Watch the goalkeeper.** To make the best possible shot, watch the goalkeeper for his level of readiness and positioning. By doing this you will be able to aim for the best possible position in the net. Look for hints such as the goalkeeper's weight distribution, the alignment relative to the goalposts, and his level of fatigue. You can also study his save history to determine the areas that he favours or avoids.

- **Weight distribution.** The goalkeeper will be moving in the goal mouth according to the movement of the ball around the goal circle. As he does so, at times he'll have his weight on one foot more so than the other. If you are ready to make a goal shot, you can fire the ball past the foot that is supporting his body weight because it will take more time for the keeper to use that foot to make a save. A firm push at goal, rather than a powerful hit to the other foot, is perhaps more useful in beating a goalkeeper whose weight is not distributed evenly. Also, the goalkeeper will try to maintain his weight in a forward position but occasionally his weight will fall backwards of centre, which also makes it difficult for him to move and react quickly in any direction.

If you notice that the goalkeeper's body weight is not on the balls of the feet (weight is not forward) but is on the heels (weight backwards), this will be a good opportunity for you to make your shot and catch the goalkeeper unaware. This is another instance in which an accurate shot when the goalkeeper is off balance can be more effective than a powerful shot when the goalkeeper is well balanced.

- **Position.** It is important for the attackers to be aware of the goalkeeper's relative positioning. The goalkeeper will position himself according to the goalposts (the posts will be the point of reference). He will look to minimise the good shooting angles for the forward. If the keeper is off line, there will be a larger gap than usual between him and the goalpost, which presents a good shooting opportunity for the forward. (This is explained further in chapter 8.)

- **Fatigue.** If the goalkeeper is required to make two or three saves in a row and has been diving for the ball, he will be fatigued. In this instance you will be well rewarded by simply getting the ball moving at goal and requiring a save. A tired goalkeeper will make a sloppy save, if any, and a shot that would otherwise be saved could sneak into goal. You can detect the goalkeeper's level of alertness by watching his body language such as his speed of movement, footwork and heavy breathing.

The goalkeeper's history of saves made will give you an idea about his strengths and weaknesses. You can research the strengths and weakness of the goalkeeper before the game in the same manner that you can for field opponents. If he has a weakness (perhaps a weak left foot or right hand), try to take advantage of this with your goal shot. Consider too the goalkeeper's agility or lack of it when deciding about which goal shot to use or whether to run around the goalkeeper and eliminate him with stick skills. The following are some general goal-shooting drills that encompass all possible shots on goal:

52   4-ON-3 DOUBLE GOAL

Purpose

To practice receiving the ball under pressure and to pass or shoot according to the best available option using all the shooting techniques discussed.

Players

Two goalkeepers, four attackers, three defenders, one passer on the baseline and one passer outside the circle or on the 25-yard line.

Procedure

Set up two goals, one at the baseline as usual and the second goal at the top of the circle or on the 25-yard line. Have a collection of balls with each of the passing players (players A and B). These players must alternate to pass to one of the attackers (players C, D, E and F) who can make a pass or shoot at either goal while the defenders (Xs) try to earn possession and pass the ball back to the player who is waiting to make the next pass into the circle (player A or B). Keep the drill flowing so that as soon as the ball is out of play or a goal is scored, the next pass is made into the circle for the next play.

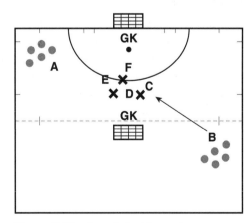

Figure 7.15   4-on-3 double goal.

Variation

This can be a 2-on-1 or a 5-on-4 situation, depending on the number of players available. (See figure 7.15.)

53   TRAP, PASS AND SHOOT UNDER PRESSURE

Purpose

To make a clean trap and pass, and then choose to either pass the ball into better position or shoot quickly when under pressure from defenders.

Players

Two to four attackers, two defenders, one goalkeeper, two passers.

Procedure

Players D and E have the balls on the baseline on either side of the goal. They alternate to hit the balls at the attackers, who make at least one pass and then shoot at goal while the defenders apply pressure. The defenders start the drill midcircle and move to apply pressure to the forwards once the pass is made from the baseline. (See figure 7.16.)

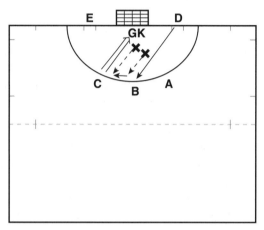

Figure 7.16 Trap, pass and shoot under pressure.

54   DOUBLE GOAL AND SHOOT

Purpose

To receive the ball and shoot quickly while maintaining vision.

Players

Two goalkeepers, one attacker, two passers (other players rotate into the drill after five shots).

Equipment

Two goals, tyres (for rebounding).

Procedure

Players A and B alternate passing the ball at player C, who shoots at goal. That player can make a decision about which goal to shoot at according to the position of the goalkeepers. Play the ball until it is out of play. (See figure 7.17.)

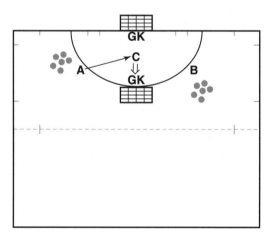

Figure 7.17 Double goal and shoot.

Goal shooting is lots of fun, and it requires the use of many skills. It is your opportunity to cash in on all your hard work and that of your team-mates. You need to have variety in your goal-shooting skills on both sides of your body and an ability to make decisions quickly according to the congestion in the circle, the situation in which you receive the ball, the readiness and positioning of the goalkeeper and, of course, your own positioning.

As always, value the initial trap so that the ball is in the best position for you to execute the next skill. Be low and alert when you prepare to receive. You may only get one or two chances to score in a game, so you need to be an opportunist—ready for a chance to put the ball in the net. Be desperate to get the ball moving towards goal, and dive if you have to!

☐ CHAPTER 8 ☐

GOALKEEPING

The goalkeepers are sometimes the quickest and most agile players in any team. They have good flexibility, are extremely brave and have quick reflexes. The goalkeeper is the last line of defence, and the play and the ball move very quickly in the important circle area. Goalkeepers, too, are usually quick to remind the field players that if they had done their jobs better, the ball would not be in the goalkeeper's territory anyway!

Goalkeeper can be a frustrating position to play at times because you need to stay focused for the whole match and may get only one or two, if any, touches during the game. Often you feel like the villain rather than the hero, and you aren't heavily involved in the play to recover from previous errors that you may have made. You won't score goals or create opportunities for others, which can bring adulation from the crowd and your team-mates.

But when it seems that only your costly mistakes are acknowledged, remember to consider all the good things that you have done that casual observers may not have recognised. The goalkeeper position has many 'low-profile' elements that can be very rewarding. For example, the tone of communication, direction and voice for the team can begin with the goalkeeper. Following is information useful for enhancing your goalkeeping skills and responsibilities, training techniques that will help you improve, and a guide to the proper equipment you'll need to keep you safe, brave and agile on the field.

Lachlan Dreher, Damon Diletti, Justine Sowry and Rachel Imison are four players who have led the way for goalkeepers worldwide. Dreher and Diletti are three-time Olympians who represented Australia for many years (22 years combined) and played almost 300 games between them. Justine Sowry is a World Cup gold medallist and currently an assistant coach and goalkeeping coach for the U.S. field hockey team. Rachel Imison is an Olympic gold medallist who still leads from the back for the Hockeyroos. Together they explain the basic skills necessary for playing in this position.

Dreher outlines the following key points, which will help you to improve your goalkeeping skills:

1. Organise your defence in the back half of the field.
2. Get to the right position in the circle as soon as you can.
3. Be steady and balanced when the shot comes.

ESSENTIAL GOALKEEPING SKILLS

The goalkeeper's role is more than a physical presence in the last line of defence. Two of the most important skills are non-physical; the ability to read and the ability and willingness to call the play quickly and decisively for the players ahead. These are roles which are critical for team cohesion and organisation, and this positive and determined tone can spread to the players further up the field. Speed, flexibility, bravery and a sound ability to make the various saves on both sides of your body are also essential for the complete goal keeper.

Reading the Play

As the deepest player on the team, the goalkeeper plays a strong role in reading and calling the play, spotting and calling attacking leads and organising the defence accordingly.

'Calls should be clear and precise and state the intended player's name first. This will attract the attention of the relevant player as quickly as possible and leave the other defensive players to concentrate on their tasks without distraction. Once you have the player's attention, you can then give the instructions.'—Damon Diletti

These are critical skills that goalkeepers can develop, just as the traditional physical skills are improved with practice.

As a goalkeeper, you have the widest view and therefore the best perspective to call the correct lines for defensive players. This will ensure good defensive organisation in the back half of the field, particularly if you make the calls in an urgent manner without sounding panicky. Also, if the goalkeeper can read the movements of teammates, he can try to rebound balls in their favour and away from the likely position of the forwards.

Diletti explains that high-quality communication from the goalkeeper can be just as useful as a good save, because with the right communication from behind, the defenders can prevent a shot on goal, which protects the goalkeeper from needing to make a save. Prevention is better than cure! Be confident and positive with your body language, even if you or one of your defenders makes a costly error.

Making Decisions

Things happen very quickly in the goal circle, so you need to be ready and able to make decisions quickly. There is no time for hesitation! The following are decisions you will encounter:

- Should I go out to meet the ball carrier or stay on the goal line?
- Should I go to the ground or stay on my feet?

1v1 situations are a good example of the need for clear and quick decision-making ability. Sowry outlines some key factors to consider when faced with a 1v1:

- Where is the player entering the circle? That is, is there a small shooting angle or a large one?
- Is pressure being applied to the ball carrier?
- Is the ball carrier in control of the ball?
- Where are the other attackers? Can the ball carrier pass around you if you confront?
- Where are the other defenders to provide the goalkeeper with support?
- How fast is the ball carrier moving, and is his head down or does he have good vision?

55 1V1S

Purpose

To provide repetition in a 'live' situation so that the goalkeeper can gain decision-making experience with a defender chasing to provide pressure for the forward. The goalkeeper also needs to call the play so that the defender is most useful to the task of defending. Calls such as 'mine' and 'cover' would be relevant here. Practice this skill from the left, centre and right of the circle, and change the direction of the ball movement as appropriate. Players include one goalkeeper and three field players. The players can rotate to experience all roles.

Procedure

The defender passes the ball to player B. Once this pass is made, the defender runs towards the circle to defend, and player C makes a lead. Player B passes the ball to the leading attacker (player C), who quickly moves towards the circle. The goalkeeper who is initially positioned midcircle defends the goal. There will be a 1v1 situation between the goalkeeper and the attacker (player C) while the defender chases to make the situation real. Practice this drill from both sides of the field and the centre of the field. (See figure 8.1.

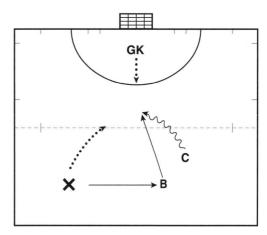

Figure 8.1 1v1.

Positioning and Angles

When the ball is upfield, begin midcircle so that you are in good position to meet an attacker at the top of the circle and you don't have far to move back to the baseline if the play is developing slowly towards you. You are also in good position to communicate with your defenders.

Dreher says that closer to home (when the ball is in the circle), many goalkeepers appear to have no idea of exactly where they are in the circle in relation to the goal. In this situation they lose their orientation because they move far too much and overreact when the ball is passed or moved around the circle. As a result, they end up off line when the shot is made, providing larger gaps than necessary between themselves and the goalposts. These gaps provide excellent opportunities for the forwards to score.

Most goals are scored not from the first shot, but from a second or third shot in rebounding situations. Therefore, the quality of the first save determines the likelihood of having to defend a crucial second shot.

The following drills will help to improve your ability to make a save and then a second save while improving your understanding of good positioning in the circle.

56   GETTING THE LINE

Purpose

To understand how to get the correct line for the shot on goal.

Procedure

Line the balls up in the circle. The goalkeeper determines the middle of the goal and draws an imaginary line from there to the ball and places a foot on either side of that line. The coach shoots at goal. Sowry suggests that occasionally it is a good idea after each save for you (the goalkeeper) to remove your gloves and place them in the position of your feet for each save; then move to where the ball was hit to see firsthand the space that was left for the shooter and to better understand what the opposing forward can see. Take your time between shots and assess each one as necessary.

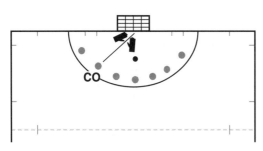

Figure 8.2   Getting the line.

Variation

Vary the shooting angle to increase the goalkeeper's understanding of the angles, or speed up the drill by shooting more quickly from alternate sides without using the gloves as markers so often. (See figure 8.2.)

57   CLEAR AND MOVE

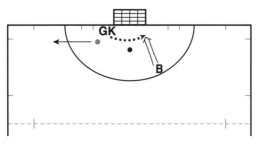

Figure 8.3   Clear and move.

Purpose

To arrive at the position to cover the angle on the second save.

Procedure

The goalkeeper begins by clearing a stationary ball out of the circle. Player B then shoots at goal, and the goalkeeper arcs around to the best position to make the save and cover the angle of what would be the second shot. (See figure 8.3.)

58 RELATIVE POSITIONING

Purpose

To practice getting into the best position considering the position in the goal and the angle of the goal shot.

Procedure

Player A passes to player B. The goalkeeper begins on the side of the ball when the first pass is made, then arcs around with the passes for the shot on goal by player C. Vary the shot type: reflex, aerial, hard and slow hits. (See figure 8.4.)

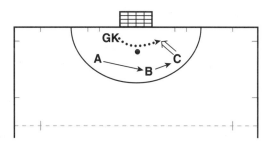

Figure 8.4 Relative positioning.

During training, a way to improve your ability to position yourself in the right place is to practice moving around the goalmouth in an arc and out of the goal box to the middle of the circle. After each of these movements, return quickly to the central position in the goalmouth and assess your end positioning.

The best position for the goalkeeper is the one that most significantly reduces the shooting angle for the forwards. As a goalkeeper, the closer to the hit you are positioned, the more you will reduce the shooting angle but the less time you will have to react to the shot on goal. You must make a compromise between proximity to the shooter and the reduction of the shooting angle you leave him, and you must assess this compromise on each occasion.

KEY NOTE
'If you are in the right place, more balls will hit you!' (Dreher)

Paul Gaudoin controls the ball in the defensive circle for Australia.

You are probably only a small change away from your correct positioning. Rarely should you need to make major changes in position. You should also be familiar with the various ground markings and use these markings to help you recognise your positioning in the circle. Examples of such landmarks or reference points include the penalty spot, the backline, the flat part at the top of the circle and the intersection of the 25-yard line and the sideline as well as the goalposts. Have a good understanding of where you are in relation to these features of the field as you move in the circle.

You can 'stay in touch' with the goalposts to help you assume the best positioning. The posts can be useful reference points if you keep your glove or stick in touch with them as you move around the goalmouth. Make contact with the posts as you move, but don't maintain that contact—they are only reference points.

Given the small confines of the circle, goalkeepers rarely need to move a great distance in one play. The movements in the goalmouth are generally over a small area using small steps to make minor adjustments. Making large steps instead of small steps to adjust is a common error that will make you slower to react to a change in the line of the ball and can also result in your failing to be on the correct line when the shot does come. It will also make you unbalanced when you need to make the save, and you'll be vulnerable to the skills of opportunistic forwards.

When the play comes into the circle along the backline, the angle for the shot is low. Sowry suggests that an angle no larger than approximately 40 degrees gives you a good opportunity to make a save because you can easily cover that small an angle. In this situation you should not be drawn to the ball carrier but should 'stay at home' in the net, unless there is a 100 percent guarantee that you will get to the ball first. Otherwise, one pass can eliminate the player in the last line of defence in this very dangerous area.

KEY NOTE
A major sign of an unbalanced goalkeeper is one who looks as though he is going to fall backwards as he makes a save. (Dreher)

Maintaining Balance

Many players have an unbalanced stance to the left or the right, or they take stuttering, nervous steps on the spot while they wait for the shot to be made. Both situations will unbalance the goalkeeper more than is necessary. After making a save and moving to adjust for a change of angles, remain stationary when the next shot is made. Remember that the clever forwards are looking for a moment to shoot when the goalkeeper is off balance even slightly or has her weight on one foot predominantly.

Using the Correct Foot

Dreher believes that many players are unable to use their non-preferred foot to save and kick the ball. As a result, they kick across the line of the ball and miss some potential saves. As a goalkeeper, you should attempt to kick up the line of the ball as it moves towards you and angle the foot to direct the ball in the path you want it to go.

If you have to swing your leg across your body to kick the ball on the non-preferred side, you are more likely to make errors and you will reduce the power that you can generate with your leg. You will also have fewer options when choosing a direction to kick or clear the ball. You won't always have time to use your preferred foot to make a save, so become proficient on both sides of your body.

Delaying the Play

Another important job for you as the goalkeeper is to delay the play until help arrives. This means that you want to hold the attacking player up (slow their attack down) while your team mates get into better defensive position to either make a tackle or to cover that of the goalkeeper.

59   DELAYING THE PLAY

Purpose

To learn to delay the attacking play or slow it down until some support arrives.

Procedure

The defender passes to player B outside the 25-yard area, then runs around the cone and tries to get back to support the goalkeeper, who quickly gets out to the top of the circle to delay the progress of the forward (player B) until help arrives. Clear communication between both defensive players (the defender and the goalkeeper) is necessary here. (See figure 8.5.)

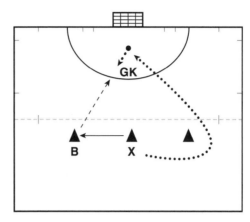

Figure 8.5   Delaying the play.

Powering Up

Women in particular tend not to put as much power as they could into their kicks and clearances. Sometimes this occurs because of the physiological differences between men and women and the different ways in which men and women play the game. (The speed and power of the shots are different, so the rebound is obviously different.) If the goalkeeper doesn't kick the ball hard, the ball will stay in and around the circle and the opposition players will be well placed to have another shot at goal or manufacture a secondary attack from the attempted clearance.

The kick can also be a pass to a team-mate. In this case the kick needs to be firm and flat. But consider that your team-mate at the other end of the pass needs to trap it, so don't necessarily kick the ball as hard as you can. Use common sense to determine the power you need to generate in each instance. The power of your kick will be determined by each situation, but as a general rule you should probably err on the side of kicking the ball too hard rather than too softly.

60   SAVE AND PASS

Purpose

To make a save and clear with accuracy and power.

Procedure

Set up a line of cones on each side of the circle. The goalkeeper makes a save and aims to hit each cone one at a time with the clearance. (See figure 8.6.)

Variation

To go for more power, move the cones back so that a firmer pass is made, or clear the ball with power between the cones.

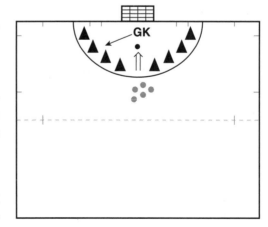

Figure 8.6   Save and pass.

Getting Physical

As noted earlier, the goalkeeper is often the most agile player on the field and, just as for the players on the field, goalkeepers must be completely competent and confident in the basic skills on both sides of their body. The following are the specific physical skills required for goalkeepers.

Instep Jab Kick

This is a controlled 'save-and-clear' technique that may also be used to pass the ball. You should open the hips to present a flat kicker at the point of contact with the ball.

Figure 8.7 Line the ball up with the centre of your instep, open your hips and present a flat kicker then 'first-time' the ball to your target. After 'jabbing' at the ball, your weight is following through in the direction of the target.

Figure 8.8 A flat kicker meets the ball wide of your body. Try to get your eyes over the ball.

Imison says that with the instep jab kick you are trying to put power back into the ball and clear it wide. This requires good timing because if you are too early to kick, you will take power out of the ball, whereas if you are too late, the ball is likely to end up in the goal.

Line the ball up with the centre of your instep to maximise your placement and ball control. As is the case for most skills, make sure your weight is going forward (in this case all your weight is going into the jab). Be sure that your head and chest are over the ball as you make contact.

For this goalkeeping technique you jab at the ball by 'first-timing' it (there is no initial stop or block) unless it is a raised shot on goal. When the shot is raised you should block it with your hand so as to guide it down to the ground before executing the clearing kick or jab. (See figure 8.7.)

Lunge Save

This is a similar technique to the instep jab, but it requires a wider stretch. You aim to make contact with the ball as outlined previously, but you will do so when the ball is wider from your body than for the jab kick. (See figure 8.8.)

As a goalkeeper, you never want to fall backwards when you make a save, so you should always attempt to make a save with your weight going forward. Dreher says that you should open the hips and get your knee over the ball at the point of contact. The wider you stretch to make a save, the more your hips come around to face the side of the field. You need good hip rotation to clear the ball wide so that your weight moves in the direction of the clearance. Because this save is wide of your midline, it is more difficult for you to achieve the perfect ball placement, but it is still possible.

Split Save

Where possible, you should have your stick or your hand out behind your foot in order to increase the distance that you can cover in front of the goal. On your right side, slide out for this save with your stick behind your leg, but be sure to get your stick to the ground first and then slide it wide along the ground with the movement of your leg. If your stick is on the ground as early as possible, you might be able to get a touch that misses your lunging leg. It is not essential for a goalkeeper to be able to do the splits because the goalkeeper will be slow to push out of that position and recover after the save is made. The split save on the left is the same. Slide your glove behind your leg to achieve the same 'backup' and lengthening effect. (See figure 8.9a-c.)

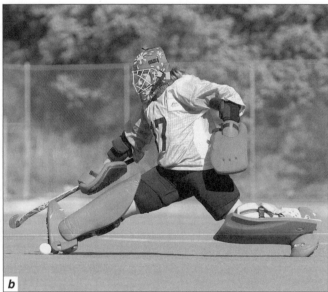

Figure 8.9 Have your stick or your hand (depending upon which side of your body the save is made) behind your foot as you split to maximise your coverage of the goal.

Air-Ball Save

To save an air ball coming straight towards you, block the ball with your glove and guide it to the ground. Once you have the ball controlled and if there is sufficient time, kick it away in a controlled manner. On the other hand, if many players are around you as you make the initial air-ball save, you can just make sure that your body is behind the ball when it drops to the ground until a defender on your team clears the ball away from the goalmouth.

An alternative to playing the ball to the ground near the goalkeeper is to deflect the ball to a safe location for the defensive team. This is easiest when the shot is struck hard and the goalkeeper simply angles the glove to direct the ball to the desired location using the pace of the initial shot. Avoid swatting the ball with the glove, which can attract the wrath of the umpire and result in a penalty stroke.

Dreher says that you'll want to do one of two things when you make a save:

- Get the ball out of the danger area by deflecting it wide of the goal or over the net.
- Keep the ball in tight control so that you can kick or push it out of the circle or a team-mate can clear it out of the danger area when the ball drops to the ground.

Figure 8.10 Head moves in the direction of the save because that keeps the torso and hips moving in that direction too.

When the ball drops to the ground, you need to control it in the least-dangerous area for the defensive team. When the ball is in the air on your right side, use the left glove instead of the stick where possible (when the ball is close to the body), as this will make the ball easier to control. You always want your head moving in the direction of the save because that keeps the torso and hips moving in that direction and enables you to achieve momentum and power. (See figure 8.10.)

Reflex Save

The best thing you can do to prepare for making these instinctive saves is to make sure that your position and balance are optimal. In this way you will be best prepared to react quickly and effectively. Control the ball wide to negate any possible danger in the second play, but don't do too much reflex-save work until your basic skills are second nature. Otherwise, you will train bad habits.

If you watch the ball, your natural reflexes will take over. Imison says that what you do after the reflex save is made is the component that you can spend time rehearsing. This is where the basic goalkeeping skills come into play. You can practice reflex saves using a coach or player to hit tennis balls with a racquet from close range.

Sliding and Stacking

Your sliding ability depends to some extent on the surface on which you play. A water-based surface means that even if your technique is not perfect, you can still execute an effective slide, whereas a sand-based surface provides more friction and resistance and requires a higher-quality slide to achieve the same effect.

You need to generate some speed as you move towards the ball and prepare to make the slide. Usually players have a preferred side (usually the right side), but you need to be able to execute this on both sides of your body. Keep your body facing the front on the approach to the ball, and as you execute the slide make sure you keep the top arm lifted above your body (to prevent a raised shot) and a little forward of the underside of your body so that you are able to maintain maximum height and balance. Be ready to get up quickly and react to the next play. Imison says you should line up the centre of your pads with the ball as you approach the ball carrier and remember to use your hands if the forward tries to drag around you. (See figure 8.11a-c.)

Figure 8.11 (*a*) Keep your body facing the front as you generate speed on approach to the ball. (*b*) As you execute the slide, keep the top arm lifted above and a little forward of your body so that you are able to maintain maximum height and balance. (*c*) Line up the centre of your pads with the ball as you approach the ball carrier and keep your top arm lifted above your body.

61   SLIDING AND DOUBLE-LEG BLOCK

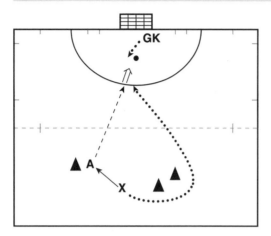

Figure 8.12   Sliding or double-leg block.

Purpose

To practice sliding and the double-leg block.

Procedure

The defender passes the ball to the attacker (player A). Player A moves towards the circle to shoot, and the defender runs around a cone and back to defend the circle and apply pressure to player A. Starting midcircle, the goalkeeper moves to slide or uses a double-leg block depending on the shooting position of player A. (See figure 8.12.)

Figure 8.13   Block the ball by standing upright and make sure you are in a stationary position and well balanced when the shot is made.

Double-Leg Block

Imison describes this blocking technique as one that is more prevalent and necessary in the women's game than in the men's game. This is because female players in general don't have the speed of their male counterparts to get to the perfect position in each situation. As a result, they can find themselves caught in 'no-man's-land'. This technique is also useful if you have made a bad decision and are caught out of position.

For the double-leg block, block the ball by standing upright. Make the first few steps as quickly as you can. When the attacker is about to execute the shot on goal, make sure you are in a stationary position and well balanced so that you can move or make a save to the left or the right if need be. The further out towards the player with the ball you can get, the more you will reduce the shooting angle. (See figure 8.13.)

Diving

As in the high-ball save, you try to block the ball with your hands or your stick because in this instance the ball is out of reach of your feet for a kick, lunge save or split save. It is a last-ditch effort to save the ball, so there is nothing to be lost by diving in this manner as long as all other (safer) saving techniques have been eliminated as possibilities. Sowry says it should always be your preference to stay on your feet for as long as possible so you are more mobile and able to make second saves and more powerful saves.

TRAINING TECHNIQUES

Training as a goalkeeper requires a multitude of specialist skills. You must be accurate with your kicking and able to execute saves and clearances with power on both sides of your body. You need to fine-tune the various physical and communication skills required for the position and make sure that other defenders participate in training drills to apply pressure to the shooting forwards so that they make decisions as they would likely make them in pressurised and real-game situations.

Knowing the Field

During training, goalkeepers can get into the habit of not dealing adequately with each ball. At training the next shot is already coming before they have dealt adequately with the previous shot, and the coach wants them to make the next save before they are ready. As a result, they practice kicking the ball straight back to where it came from or make an inadequate save, which they wouldn't necessarily (and don't want to) do in a match situation.

Drills don't always allow enough time for you to do otherwise because the drill is not always for the benefit of the goalkeeper entirely, and the forwards are quickly generating the next attack. The coach also wants more practice in the time available, so the next attack is on the way before the last is complete for the goalkeeper. The main thing is for the goalkeeper to focus on completing one save at a time, not dealing half-heartedly with each because the next is already on the way. Sowry says that if the coach and players are intent on quickly moving onto the next play, the goalkeeper should not be concerned with making that next save; rather, he should focus on completing the initial save and be prepared to sacrifice the next shot.

For each drill that involves the goalkeeper and forwards, play each out to completion so that the drill is not over until the ball leaves the circle. Either the ball is cleared by the goalkeeper and defenders out of the circle or a goal is scored or the forwards miss the net. Until one of these occurs, play on, and all players will get maximum benefits from the drill.

In the drills, you should include the goalkeeper in all explanations so that he understands what the other players are trying to achieve from the drill. Often the goalkeeper is isolated from the group, which limits his ability to learn about the game from an attacking perspective (these are the players the goalkeeper will come up against) and defensive position (these are the players he will be working with and calling).

EQUIPMENT

For your safety and agility as a goalkeeper, you need well-fitting equipment. You must be able to move freely and have the necessary items for your level of play. For example, if you are playing senior men's hockey you will not find that junior equipment provides adequate protection. If you are not adequately protected you will feel unsafe, be at risk for injuries and find it difficult to be brave at the critical moment. The required basic equipment is as follows (see figure 8.14):

- Pads
- Kickers
- Chest protector

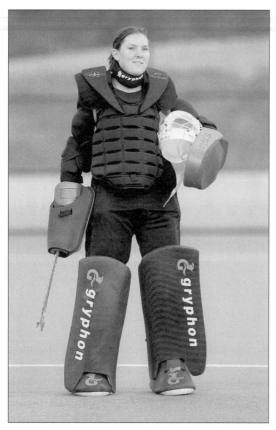

Figure 8.14 Necessary protective gear for the goalkeeper.

- Groin protector for men or pelvic protector for women
- Helmet
- Gloves
- Elbow pads
- Throat protector

If you have confidence in your equipment, you will feel safe and be able to concentrate on making the necessary save. Once you have been hit by the ball a couple of times you will realise that it doesn't hurt and you can concentrate on making your saves.

Inexperienced goalkeepers sometimes are afraid of the ball, particularly if it is lifted towards the upper body or the head. To avoid injury, always face the front (never turn your back). Protective equipment for goalkeeping protects the front of the body, so keep that part of your body facing the ball. Duck your chin if the ball is moving towards your face and you can't get out of the way. A save with the helmet is still a save!

Of all the positions on the field, goalkeeping is the most specialised, which is why I have focused so strongly on the advice of the experts. The physical attributes, equipment and skills for goalkeepers are completely different than those for the field players. Appropriate equipment is important because if you are not well protected, you will (rightly) hesitate! It is also important for the drills to be safe and realistic so that you have the best chance of developing into a confident goalkeeper.

Positioning within the goal and the circle is important, so use the points of reference discussed in this chapter so that you know where you are in the circle. Be sure to take your time to rehearse your skills in drills that are specific to your position so that you do not rush the save for the sake of the drill. If this is not possible, make a conscious effort to complete your task (save and clear) before looking for the next save. Much of your job is to organise and control your defence as well as make saves using the physical skills we have discussed, so practice doing this during training drills.

Goalkeeping is a very rewarding and enjoyable position to play, but it isn't for everyone! It is a critical position so a great performance will be valued highly by your team-mates. You can make a positive difference for your team because a great save is as important as a goal scored by your forwards at the other end of the field.

PLAYING THE GAME

In part I you explored the basic skills of the game in isolation. At this point, you may have the physical tools to play the game but no framework to help you apply them in actual game.

Part II considers the physical and non-physical skills and teamwork considerations that make up your team's method of play. In combination with the skills presented in part I, these supplementary elements of the game will help you become a more complete team player.

Most of the components for discussion in part II are specific to team play. They include the important factor of communication, the significant role of set plays (including penalty corners in attack and defence), the alternative styles of play, the various attacking and defensive strategies, and of course the ever-critical (and much-maligned) area of fitness for the game of hockey. Without a certain level of fitness you will be unable to get onto the field to use your skills and help the team achieve its goals and you will be vulnerable to injury. Similarly, unless you learn to communicate successfully with the players on your team, you will find it difficult to fit successfully into the group and maximise your contribution—no matter how skilled you are as an individual. Your individual style of play should be consistent with the objectives of the group, so you will need to tailor your game to play appropriately according to those group goals and ideals.

Part II also explains some practical scenarios to help you showcase those skills you have developed, while complementing the skills and strengths of others within the group. Consistency and team orientation are based on a clear understanding of each player's role within the team, but the extent to which each player is able to apply this theory on the field will determine his or her progress as a team player.

It is one thing to be highly skilled as an individual, but hockey is a team sport that requires coordination amongst each of the players on a team. Bear this in mind as you set about developing your game, and you will be well on your way to becoming the best field hockey player that you can be.

☐ **CHAPTER 9** ☐

TEAM COMMUNICATION

The ball moves very quickly in the game of hockey, perhaps more quickly and more frequently than for most other sports. Because it is a fluid game and the playing environment changes so quickly, communication among the players on a team is particularly important. Everything you do at training and on the field during a match should reflect the goals and ambitions of your team. Remember—a successful team is greater than the sum of its parts!

The following discussion points consider the components that are most important for your development as a player within a competitive team. You should communicate clearly, learn to play from the bench, be persistent, and learn to prepare for all those 'what-ifs'.

ORIENTATION AND COMMUNICATION

Know where you are on the field in relation to the other players on your team, and know where you are positioned in relation to the opposition players. This may seem obvious, but the smallest step to the left or the right can make a big difference to the positions of the players on your team who are setting up behind you. Small changes in position can significantly change the passing angles available to your opponents also.

Often the other players make positional judgements and calls for you, and you should trust that the players behind you have the best view of the field. Be confident that their instructional calls (left or right, for example) are based on a better view of the field than yours.

You have a view of only the players in front of you and in your immediate area, whereas the players behind you can see the bigger picture, including a larger portion of the field. It is not only what you say to surrounding players, but also the tone of voice you use that is significant. A panicked call to a team-mate can be contagious; this feeling will quickly spread amongst your team-mates. A calm directional call will leave the player you are calling to concentrate on important things other than his positioning, such as making a good trap, a pass or an instinctive interception.

Panicked calling is also encouraging for the opposition, who will sense that things are not going well for you. That might be the little encouragement they need to improve their own game or discover a new sense of enthusiasm that can spread just as quickly through the opposition team, just as the negativity will amongst yours.

When you're setting up lines or a press up the field, the calls will usually come from behind you, from the players who have the best view of the field. The calls will serve at least one of two purposes: calls for information and direction, and calls for encouragement and recognition.

Information and Direction

These calls are from team-mates who in effect are your extra eyes when you are in possession of the ball, or perhaps even when you are setting up your position for the next play. This communication provides extra information about the playing environment. It is very useful for the ball carrier as well as for other players who have most of the field behind them as they set up the defensive press.

Some examples of calls for information are as follows:

- 'Two steps right,' 'She's on your left' or 'Hold there.'
- An attacker coming to support the ball carrier may call, 'On your left,' 'Space on your right' or 'You have time.'
- 'Hold possession.'

Players behind the ball carrier have good vision of the field ahead and can give the player with the ball information about the location of open spaces, the location of the nearest opponent, the location of the best pass, and the time available to execute the pass. Players behind the ball carrier give information that the other player is not in a position to have otherwise because of pressure and a necessary preoccupation with other areas of the game.

Australia's Brent Livermore (left) and Michael McCann talk tactics.

At the Commonwealth Games in Kuala Lumpur in 1998, we were training at the stadium at which we were to play our first game. It was an evening session and about halfway through, the lights went out and we assumed that the session would be called off. Not to be! We played a small half game in the dark, relying almost entirely on the calls and information given by team-mates. This unusual and unplanned training session emphasised to us just how important it is to make clear, calm and decisive calls to team-mates. The calls, both instructional and informative, provided us with just about all the available information.

62 SILENT HOCKEY

Purpose

To emphasise the importance of calling in normal game situations and to emphasise the need for players to make definitive leads.

Procedure

Set up a small game-situation, but the players are not allowed to communicate using their voices. The ball carrier will find it more difficult to make decisions without the verbal help of the players around him. There will be many turnovers in this drill because the important verbal communication component of the game has been removed.

Encouragement and Recognition

These calls are important communicating tools, because often some players are 'off' their game and need encouragement to get back to their best. Also, on some occasions players have made good efforts but have narrowly missed a target or not quite won a contest with opponents, and they can become disheartened. Positive communication and encouragement are useful here. Similarly, team-mates, coaches and players watching from the bench can offer with positive reinforcement for excellence in skill execution. Be careful not to overlook this important component of the game. Every little bit helps!

PLAYING FROM THE BENCH

Critical to the Hockeyroos' success over a long period was the fact that the group had an enormous depth of talent and therefore an ability to rotate players on and off the field to maximise the intensity that was so damaging to other teams. If you have a good depth of talent in your team you don't need to name a regular 'first 11'; you can simply rest and rotate the starting side and be confident of a good result. The smaller the gap in ability between your best and weakest players, the better your chance of implementing this rotational concept so that your team maintains the quality of its play.

The role of the bench player is important in a team situation. Try to see your time on the bench as an opportunity to recover physically, recap mentally and prepare for your next intensive stint. If you rotate on and off the bench you will be in good shape to maintain the high-intensity game that is so damaging.

There are many reasons that your coach may take you from the field. It may be that you are being rested for a future match, you need a break so that you can return to the field after the break and generate a higher intensity of play, you are out of form and would benefit from a break or the coach may be trying a new player or a new combination of players in your area of the field. Perhaps a player has a specialist role in the penalty-corner battery and needs to be on the field during a particular stage of the match because your team really needs to score.

This down time is an opportunity for you to sit back and watch your opponent without the pressure of performing skills at the same time. Also, it is a chance to support your team-mates with positive calling and encouragement and to communicate with other players whom you have been playing with. This is also a time when you can talk with your coach about the way you and the team are performing and the messages you can take back to the players on the field when you return. Remember, this down time is not the time for you to 'spit the dummy' because you have been taken from the field. No one likes coming off the field, but this is a necessary part of being a valuable team player.

At times you may be required to play out of your regular position. This means that because of an injury, form slump or other factors occurring amongst the players around you, you will need to play in a position that is not your favourite or the one you consider your strongest. You and the players on your team need to be flexible enough in their ability and mind-set that they can do this comfortably and without much notice.

DEFINING YOUR POSITION

There is more to the game than mastering physical skills. Responsibility for your performance and that of the team, having an adventurous, brave, positive and proactive attitude will also make you and the team stronger. Self-analysis, honesty and leadership are also such non-physical skills and attributes which are useful for team players to develop just as persistence when things are not going to plan and planning for potential scenarios are too.

Be Responsible for Your Game

Don't be a robot. Own your game, make brave decisions and be responsible for your performance and actions. This is an area on which we all need to concentrate occasionally, particularly when things aren't going to plan. If you take the attitude that you own your game and that there are responsibilities that go with that attitude—things that only you can control—you will find that your game improves more quickly than it does for the players who blame external factors such as other players, the crowd, the surface or the coach when all is not going smoothly. These variables are part of the game, and you should not use them as an excuse for substandard performances. They are simply factors you must accept and work around, just as every other player on the field must.

To own your game is to be accountable to criticism and evaluation of your performance without pointing your finger at people or things that potentially prevent you from playing at your best. It may sound like an oversimplification, but chances are the moment you stop looking for excuses about why things are not going to plan, you will recognise the skill or decision-making errors that are letting you down, and you can improve them for next time.

The really good players react in a positive manner when things are not going to plan. It is easy to play well and be a good team player when things are going well, but it is more difficult to turn difficult situations around and remain a positive influence when things aren't going as planned. Everyone falls into this trap occasionally, but beware the players who always default to this style, particularly those who refuse to look to themselves to make improvements and turn things around.

Similarly, once you are out on the field, you have to make decisions for yourself. The coaching staff can guide you at training, before the game or at half-time, but they can't make decisions for you out on the field. Players need to react to bad umpiring decisions, bad luck and other variables, so be ready to make positive decisions based on your own preparation, experiences and beliefs. Prepare as well as possible, keep a cool head and act with conviction. If you do make mistakes, and you certainly will, learn from them and make sure you do better next time.

First you must recognise that you have made an error, then you can fix it for next time. If you look only for external reasons to explain why errors occur, the errors are likely to continue to be a feature of your game.

KEY NOTE
We often learn more from mistakes than we do from success. Re-evaluation is necessary in this case, not optional!

Learn to Be a Leader

Beware the tempting attitude that the players' responsibilities begin and end with the captain. Try to have 11 leaders on the field at any given time so that you don't wait to be told what to do and when to do it. Each player can take responsibility for the game situation and make the necessary changes. It may be that an opposition player is injured and your team is momentarily one player up. Each player needs to recognise this situation and be willing to communicate it to the rest of the team as quickly as possible. It shouldn't be left to the nominated captain to recognise it (he or she might be off the field at that time), because such a development can present a good offensive opportunity. The team that most quickly recognises and capitalises on opportunities when they arise most often wins.

Everyone can lead by example whether by running hard, encouraging team-mates or calling in a positive tone. In the lead-up to the Olympic Games in Sydney, we didn't have a formally appointed captain. That official role and the role of the vice captain were rotated amongst all the players in the playing group, which meant that each player was ultimately responsible for the performance and development of the team. We also had several players at any one time who would take a leading role on the field as necessary.

Be Flexible

Learn to be a flexible player and an adventurous player, and you will be a valuable team player. This is an important point for players who are trying to break into representative teams, and I am sure the principle applies in many sports. Usually 10 or 12 players in each hockey team are automatic selections week in and week out, with the remaining team members fighting for selection on the basis of features of their game other than their ability to play in their primary position.

In 1996 when the Olympic team was selected, I was certainly not in the automatic selection group, and ultimately my non-selection for the Olympic team came down to my inability (compared with other players) to play more than one position with great skill. The final selections usually come down to team balance, so your ability to play out of your line (striker line, midfield line, defence line) will be important considerations, just as your ability to perform certain specialised tasks such as penalty corner skills will be significant. Understand the various positions, and make yourself available to give them a go, even at training or for small patches during games. It will make you a more valuable player, and it will help you at the selection table.

Don't be afraid to make mistakes and try new skills, because if you aren't doing so, you're probably not extending yourself as a player. You will improve by introducing and refining new skills in game situations, so be brave and have a go. We have discussed the idea that it is necessary to try new skills, but your sense of adventure in this regard will also make you a more flexible and a more valuable player. The only way to develop your skills for a game situation is to practice them in that environment. It is one thing to be able to execute a skill perfectly at training, but it is another thing entirely to achieve the same result in a pressurised game situation. Be brave!

In a match situation you have less time to think about the skill execution than you do in a training environment. You need to recognise appropriate situations in which to use the skill; you need to consider variables such as the varied positions of your opponents and team-mates. You may only have one opportunity to get a result, which adds to the pressure of getting it right the first time.

In a training session you have the benefit of being able to have another go when you make a mistake, and this knowledge will take the pressure off. If you can execute a particular skill regularly in a game situation, then that is a good sign that you are becoming proficient in that skill. The only certainty when trying new skills is that you will make mistakes. If you are not making errors you are probably not extending yourself to learn and be the best you can be. As long as you learn from your mistakes and recognise your weaknesses, there is no reason you shouldn't introduce new skills to your game. Get out of the comfort zone! New skills will also help you at the selection table.

Think It Through

Players often have unrealistic expectations of themselves in a game situation. If this is the case, you will often leave the field feeling frustrated. Make your objectives simple and achievable. Be ambitious, but make your goals achievable. Your goals for a match might be as follows:

- Give the simple pass when I see it.
- Turn and chase immediately if I lose possession.
- Get to the goalpost every time the ball enters the attacking circle.

Think about possible situations you might find yourself in before the game. You can anticipate those situations, so prepare for the possibilities as much as you can. You can analyse the strengths and weaknesses of likely opponents and match conditions, the temptation to fall into old habits when under pressure and crowd and weather distractions, just to name a few. Often if you acknowledge possible difficulties early, they will be of little or less consequence during the course of a game because you will already have determined the best course of preventive or alternative action.

I mentioned the weather because if it has been raining heavily, the field will be slow. If the field is slow and you and your team ordinarily play a fast-running game, you will be frustrated by your inability to move the play quickly and run with the ball—that is, unless you make a plan to change your style of play. Instead of running with the ball, pass the ball by lifting it slightly above the surface of the field. Overheads are a good option too.

- Be smart and adapt to the conditions rather than fight them. Conditions are the same for both teams!

- Know your opponent. Before each game you will often know who your immediate opponent is, so be aware of their strengths and weaknesses and play accordingly. Eat well in the lead-up to a game and training sessions, and hydrate appropriately. Even if the conditions are cold, make sure you take in plenty of water before the match, and have plenty available to replace the fluids you lose in the course of the game.

- The most important point is to enjoy the game, the training sessions and the experience of playing in a team environment. It is lots of fun!

- Control the controllables and don't worry about anything else. This is my favourite saying; however, it is easier said than done! It is easy in a competitive environment to get caught up in what everyone else is doing and lose focus on the areas on which you need to concentrate. This is draining and wastes energy because largely these are factors you have no control over.

But as a competitive player, often you will worry about these uncontrollables. It may be that you are trying to earn a position in a team, and you are wasting time and energy worrying about how well another player in the same position (someone you are competing against) is playing. On the other hand, you may be concerned about how well your opposition team is playing. This is perfectly natural. In both scenarios, there is nothing you can do to influence these external factors—just concentrate on your own game. If young players ever ask me for advice, I always suggest that they put their time and effort into 'controlling the controllables'—don't waste your time worrying about things that you can't control.

Recognise that you are wasting your energy on these thoughts, and concentrate on things you can control. Don't worry about what everyone else is doing. If there is one thing I have learned from my time as an athlete, it is that no amount of worry about things you can't control can have a positive effect on your own game. You will only become more drained of energy and more nervous, and this cannot translate positively to your game.

BEING PERSISTENT

Rarely does a sporting career continue smoothly from beginning to end. Obstacles might come in the form of injury, slumps in form, selection issues, fluctuating motivation, and disappointment.

- **Injury.** Sometimes injuries are unavoidable, but you can take measures to prevent some injuries and speed up your rehabilitation when they do occur. A high level of fitness, attention to warm-ups and cool-downs, hydration and diet all contribute to injury prevention. (These factors are discussed further in chapter 14.)

It is tempting to go back to training too early in competitive team environments because the players are so concerned about losing their position to someone else or losing form or match fitness. In some situations the medical staff are best suited to make the call about your suitability to play, because they are emotionally removed from the situation. You will be eager to get back to the game if you have been injured, but it may not be in your long-term interest or the interest of the team for you to do so.

- **Form slump.** All players perform at a certain range within their ability, and at some stages all players fall short of what they consider a good performance. The important thing to remember (or have someone remind you of) in this situation is that you don't lose your skills and ability overnight. There can be many reasons for a slump in form, but usually if you recognise the symptoms early, you can turn things around soon enough. Get back to the basics of the game, execute those skills well and you will soon get back to form. But beware the temptation to do too much and overcompensate for your mistakes. Again, keep it simple.

- **Selection issues.** Team selection is subjective in nature. In the case of individual sports, the athletes can do a qualifying time or throw a particular distance to earn selection, but in team sports the players need to fit into a certain style and have particular individual skills that fit well with the other players in the group.

Of course, on some occasions a coach might seem to dislike your style of play. That doesn't mean you are not a good player; it simply means that you should talk to the coach about your game and make the appropriate adjustments. Whatever you do, don't be scared to ask the hard questions of the coaching staff because you will more quickly determine the solution to your problem and determine a positive course of action rather than dwell on the negatives, which will only limit your improvement.

Even if you are playing well, you might still be overlooked because the selectors are looking for team balance rather than your good form in isolation. Perhaps the coaches need a player who plays more than one position or executes a specialist skill, more than they need a player who is in form. In our team, very few players participated in all major tournaments for which they were available.

• **Fluctuating motivation.** Try to work out the reasons for your fluctuating motivation. Maybe you need time away from the training track, maybe you have plenty of other things in your life that are dominating your energy for the moment, or you may not be having the success on the field that you had hoped for. Talk to the players on your team and your coach and support staff, and find a way of changing the things you are doing so that you become refreshed and enthusiastic again.

• **Disappointment.** You should be disappointed with substandard performances, but it is only sport, after all. Sport is not always about winning. If it were, there would be many disgruntled players. Work on the areas of the game that need improving, but try not to be too disconsolate when you don't have a win, and enjoy the experience of playing with a team and the little successes that you have along the way such as improving a particular skill or set plays anyway.

At disappointing times, you need to persist. If you gave up at the first hurdle, your career would be very short—just look at any successful athlete and you will probably notice that they have had their ups and downs too! If you are motivated enough to improve your game, you will overcome the obstacles as they occur. If it is any comfort, know that most other players have been through similarly tough times. You aren't the first, and you certainly won't be the last to be in these situations!

If you set your mind to being the best player you can be, prepare yourself to encounter the inevitable and numerous hurdles along the way. Whether you want to play in the highest level of competition in your city, or you have ambition to represent your country at a World Cup or an Olympic Games, you have to be persistent and committed to the tough times as well as to the good times.

CONQUERING THE WHAT-IFS

You, your team-mates and coaches can spend many hours discussing the scenarios that may occur over the course of a match or a tournament. These may be philosophical discussions about what is wrong and right, or they may be practical decisions that you need to make over the course of the match or a tournament.

Each player needs to be clear in his or her mind about the team's response to particular situations. As national squad members, we allocated lots of time to determining our course of action in various situations. We talked over the following scenarios:

• What is the team's response if the umpire makes an incorrect decision in regard to awarding a goal in our favour? As a team, should we claim the goal or tell the umpire what actually occurred and that the goal should not count?

• What should we do if the opposite situation occurs and our team is penalised by an incorrect decision? It may be that the captain or another previously nominated player is the one to approach the umpire in this instance.

• Australian teams over the last decade or so have developed variations of a 'situation index', which would include situations such as those in figure 9.1. These situations are examples only. Your team can develop your own.

Figure 9.1 Situation Index

1. **Your team scores a goal.**

   Immediately try to play in your opponent's defensive half.

   Press aggressively as a unit.

   Eliminate risks in defence.

   Value possession.

   Maintain intensity.

2. **Your opponent scores a goal.**

   Play the way you intended to, have belief in what you are doing and don't blame anyone.

   Consider a 'power play' to gain territorial advantage whereby at the restart of the match two players dribble and pass between each other down the middle of the field to gain territory.

   Look to take advantage of a relaxed attitude of your opposition.

   Value possession and maintain a secure defensive zone.

3. **Opponents use overheads.**

   Get there first and aim to win possession.

   Get under the ball.

   Forwards put increased pressure on the players most likely to execute this skill to shut them down.

4. **Opponents play through one side in attack.**

   If their play is predominantly down the right side, your left-side players make their defensive role the priority more so than usual.

   Press up the field and mark to deny the opponent space.

   Encourage them to move the ball to the left side using the press.

   Make their right-side support players defend when they are dispossessed.

   Play your game.

5. **Opponents hit long balls to strikers.**

   Deep defenders play close to their striker and make a contest every time.

   Midfielders stretch back and cover lines where appropriate.

   Defenders communicate with each other.

   Delay tackling by deep defender until defensive support arrives.

   Defend as a unit.

   Condense the midfield so that they are forced to hit wide.

6. **Umpires call stoppages for suspensions and injury.**

   Get together as a group to get team messages out and maximise the opportunity to communicate with other team members.

   Assess the situation and make tactical changes if you lose a player through suspension or injury.

   Take time to get information from the bench.

   Rehydrate if possible.

(continued)

7. **Your team has a breakaway forward.**

Other forwards make every effort to get there and help to receive a pass or jump on a rebound.

Don't stand back and watch.

Break away player to get a quality shot or a penalty corner or make a pass to a team-mate, depending on the situation. If outnumbered and the previous outcomes are not possible, hold possession until support arrives.

Defenders on your team push up but look around at your opponent's attacking possibilities if the ball is turned over.

Communicate the situation ahead to the ball carrier, who may not have the necessary focus on the play and position of players ahead.

8. **Your opponent has a breakaway forward.**

The relevant players make every effort to get back and defend no matter how hopeless the situation seems; you might end up in position to collect the resulting spillage if the play breaks down.

Getting back puts pressure on the ball carrier, even if you are not in good position to make a tackle.

Channel the ball carrier wide or upset her ball control by distracting her.

If the goalkeeper is committed to the player with the ball, get into a cover position behind the goalkeeper to make the last line of defence.

All players must communicate their positions and intentions with each other.

9. **Your team leads by one goal with two minutes to run on the clock.**

Keep possession in your attacking half of the field.

Hit the ball from defence to gain territory and keep the ball out of your defensive area. Make sure to hit through a certain gap, use an overhead, transfer the ball to the other side of the field or hit over the sideline as a last resort.

If territory is gained, press up and be diligent about your marking roles and be aware of opposition high strikers' positions.

Maintain composure.

10. **Ten minutes to go and your team is behind.**

Concentrate on the task at hand and don't be distracted by the potential outcome.

Hold possession and attack appropriately to win a penalty corner.

Tackle, chase and press with conviction.

Do not let them score.

Remember that they are tired too. If you play the way you have rehearsed, believe that you will make a couple of chances.

11. **Reasons for interchange.**

Rest because of fatigue or heat.

Change tactics.

Receive tactical instructions.

If you're out of form, this can be an opportunity to refocus.

A set-play expert is required on the field.

A player is suspended, so others have to reshuffle.

12. **You are being marked closely or tagged.**

Concentrate on winning the ball off the opposition by making interceptions and tackles.

Rotate position with other players.

Keep things simple.

Ask yourself if you are leading well enough or are making yourself available. If not, make a change.

Take your immediate opponent out of the play when appropriate. Even if you don't have the ball, you can still influence the play.

13. **Your team is in good form or you are in good form.**

Keep doing the basic skills well (trapping, passing, tackling, leading and calling).

Keep it simple.

Don't flirt with form!

14. **Your team is out of form or you are out of form.**

Focus on getting the elements of your game functioning again.

Focus on the immediate task and don't get bogged down with the outcome.

Remember what it feels like to be in form.

Remember that you don't lose your skills overnight; they will come back if you persist and focus on doing the simple things well.

15. **Your team is one player down because of injury or suspension.**

Organise your structure so that your team is defensively sound.

Make the appropriate interchanges to cover the deficit—you may play without a striker temporarily.

Be sure that the work rate of the group is as high as possible.

Initial movement of forwards into defensive is vital, so make sure these players get the defensive goal side of the free hit.

Increase the value of possession, and reduce the risks taken offensively and defensively.

16. **Your team is one player up (your opposition is one player down).**

Value possession and make them chase and get tired.

Use the width of the field and move the ball quickly.

Beware the temptation to relax and think that things will be easy. For this reason, teams often score when they are a player down.

Maintain the game plan.

17. **One of your defenders is overlapping from defence.**

Another player must cover him defensively.

All players are alert for possible developments.

Keep leading.

Support the overlapping player by being available for a pass.

Communicate with the player about the cover situation so that they can commit to their offensive move without undue concern for the defensive role.

(continued)

18. Opposition player overlaps.

Don't rush at the player; delay the play.

Make a stopping tackle if necessary (you are outnumbered).

Be ready to punish the player defensively if you can get possession.

19. Your team is blocked in the defensive zone by their press.

Use overheads strategically.

Take free hits quickly to make the most of the space available.

Use a small touch so that the hitter can move with the ball and draw the opponents and hit through that line.

Have players in front of their press to help the ball through when your player is hitting it upfield.

Transfer the ball with speed and tempo to make your opponents shift and make spatial changes.

20. Conditions are hot and you are tired.

Limit turnovers; value possession.

Use positive self-talk.

Keep things simple.

Do things rather than wait for someone else to do them.

Break the play down to slow it down.

Use interchange players.

Concentrate on getting set plays right.

21. Your team is 3-0 up at half-time.

Maintain your work rate.

Don't overplay the ball (don't try to do too much or be too clever).

Continue to make chances.

Continue to chase and recover.

Keep doing the things that gave you the lead.

22. Your team is down 3-0 at half-time.

Make sure no further goals are scored against you.

Create offensive chances.

Maintain pressure and continue to press aggressively.

Maintain a solid defensive unit.

Stay positive and calm; make yourself useful.

Focus on the team play.

Use the space ahead when it is there.

Hockey is a team game, so you need to be a player (or a coach) who makes life easier for the other players in the group. Doing so will improve the performance of your team. As is the case for any group in all situations, clear, honest and positive communication is necessary in order for the team to best do its job and achieve the goals of the group. Communication can be in the form of verbal instruction and encouragement or body language that sets a tone for your team and gives a deliberate message to your opponents.

Each player can work to become more flexible and useful as a team member on and off the field and responsible and better prepared for the eventualities. Accept that you will make mistakes, and learn from them (both your own and those of the team) because they can be valuable learning tools. Trust the players around you, be persistent when you are challenged by the perceived obstacles to your progress and take responsibility for your own performance and that of the team. This will help you improve more quickly and make you a better player and a more valuable team member. Again, if the team does well, then likely so will you!

CHAPTER 10

STYLES OF PLAY

The styles of play that you adopt will largely reflect the number of players you want to allocate to defence, midfield and attack at any given time. You will have 11 players on the field at one time, and the starting positions on the field will not differ much, no matter which style you adopt. The differences between the styles will be more obvious as players commit more or less to attacking and defensive roles during the course of the game. Whatever your team adopts, nothing is set in stone. You can always make changes according to your opposition, the form of particular players, playing conditions and, perhaps most significant, the score line.

When you are evaluating styles of play for your team to adopt, determine your individual and team strengths and weaknesses. Define your team goals and plan your defensive and attacking set-ups accordingly. Will you use an aggressive press, zone, man-to-man or a combination of them all? When you recognise your main method of scoring as a team you are likely to play a style that complements that strength.

DETERMINING STRENGTHS AND WEAKNESSES

Is your goal all-out attack, or is it defence and a clean net at all costs? Is your goal to play patient hockey while waiting for a counterattacking opportunity because you don't think you can win using another tactic? Or is it impulsive and attacking hockey that creates risks defensively but creates lots of scoring opportunities?

It may be that you have a strong penalty-corner battery and are simply looking to win penalty corners from which you think your team has a good chance to score. This will mean that you don't need to commit large numbers of players to attack because you are not necessarily trying to score field goals. You can keep numbers in the midfield and work the ball upfield, slowly but surely. This is not necessarily a pretty or fast style of hockey to watch, but it can be effective with the appropriate personnel on your corner battery. Many teams consider a penalty corner to be a free shot on goal, so they play to win penalty corners. For example, currently the Pakistan men's team has a particularly effective flicker, Sohail Abbas, so a penalty corner for that team is particularly useful.

Similarly, you might have fast players in your team who are very good at executing the counterattacking style of play. In this instance it may be that your midfielders and strikers are quick to break in the right situation, so your team defends stoutly and waits for the right moment to make one of very few attacking moves during a match. The English women's team usually has speedy strikers who they often rely on in this way, and the U.S.A women's team tries to score through the counterattack predominantly also.

It may be that you have the personnel to absorb attacking pressure for the duration of the game and seize one of very few attacking opportunities when it arises. Spain is a team in women's hockey that does this in the extreme, and the United States occasionally does too. In this situation you would commit many players to defensive roles and sit only one or two strikers up high to receive the ball and win a penalty corner or get a good goal shot away when and if the opportunity arises as the result of an opposition error. This style you might adopt if you didn't think you could reliably match the opposition for skill and possession for the duration of the game. In this instance you would have the attitude:

'Player for player we probably don't have the personnel to win, so we'll defend and hope we can get a scoring opportunity against the run of play.' This is a perfectly common, legitimate and effective game plan that will frustrate your opposition!

John Mowat is one noteworthy coach that I had for many years. Mowat, an FIH coach and VIS head coach of the men's program, believes the most difficult component is the important decision-making aspect of the game.

Mowat says the style of play that you choose for your team (and this may change according to the state of play) will depend predominantly on three factors:

1. The strengths and weaknesses of your team, and your predominant method of scoring

2. The strengths and weaknesses of your opposition, and their predominant method of scoring

3. Your preferences and experiences learned as a coach or a player, which influence your decisions in all areas of the game

The style of play that you choose might differ according to the particular opposition on any given day and the strengths and weaknesses of both teams. The most basic choices that you have in regard to a system or a style are as follows, although it is important to keep in mind that variations are available for each of these. Toni Cumpston, head women's coach of the VIS, makes the following general observations about the basic styles of play.

Traditional Style of Play

This traditional system often appears more in practice as follows:

- Five forwards, three halfbacks, two deep defenders, one goalkeeper (figure 10.1a)
- Two high strikers, three midfielders (inside forwards), three halfbacks, two fullbacks, one goalkeeper (figure 10.1b)

- Three high strikers, two attacking midfielders, three defensive midfielders, two defenders, one goalkeeper (figure 10.1*c*)
- Two high strikers, two attacking midfielders, two defensive midfielders, four defenders, one goalkeeper (figure 10.1*d*)
- Four high strikers, two midfielders, three defenders and an attacking sweeper in front of the defenders, rather than behind in the traditional sense (figure 10.1*e*)

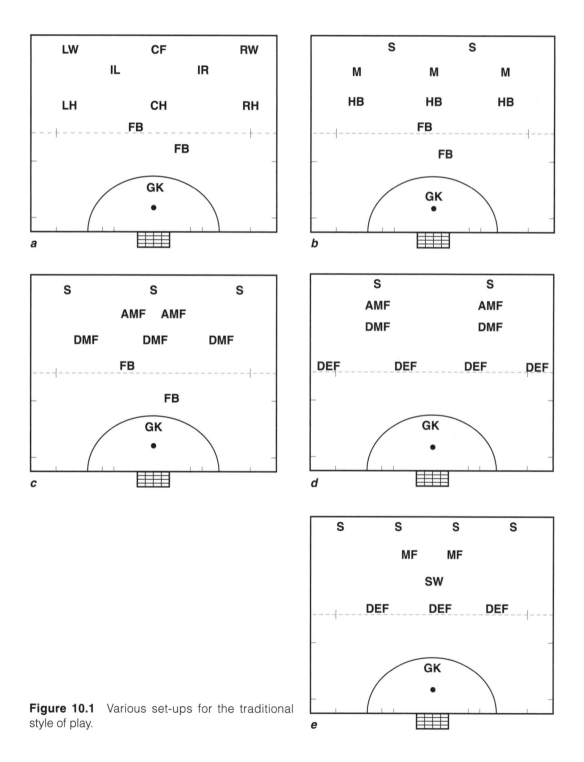

Figure 10.1 Various set-ups for the traditional style of play.

This is the traditional Australian or Eastern set-up that has an emphasis on attack. When a team is in possession of the ball, this style enables them to get numbers into attack and encourages the use of width and depth to stretch the opposition's defence. When a team is not in possession of the ball, there is man-to-man marking on the side of the ball, with the defenders on the opposite side of the field providing cover defence. This traditional style of play is more attacking in nature than the alternatives and would be used by a team that is solid at the back and also strong in attack.

European Style of Play
The formation of three strikers, three midfielders, three defenders, one deep defender and one goalkeeper is typically a European style of play, which emphasises having numbers in midfield. It is a safe option and minimises the risk of your opponents' breaking and attacking with numbers through the midfield. (See figure 10.2.)

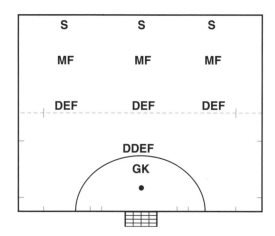

Figure 10.2   The European style of play.

The European style emphasises possession and control of the play. When in possession of the ball, players usually pass the ball around in a 'stick-to-stick' manner rather than throwing it into space. By doing this, players expect that the ball movement will create opportunities and space in the opponent's positional lines to enable forwards to receive the ball in a one-on-one situation without a cover defence in place.

When a team does not have possession, the emphasis with the European style of play is on man-to-man defence, with the central defender acting as sweeper and offering cover from in front of or behind the other defenders. The majority of teams play with a combination of these systems. In this situation the result is that most teams value possession and pass the ball around 'stick to stick' until a good opportunity is created or gaps open up, allowing weighted balls to be passed through the lines for running attackers. The defensive structure enables defence to support the attack without the risk of being exposed because of lack of cover.

These styles of play are indicative only. The important thing to remember is that the players must understand the exact way in which they are to play their positions on the field, not only the format in which they are to line up on the field. For example, each player's role within the particular style will differ slightly according to the playing conditions, the opposition and the team objectives.

KEY NOTE
The best form of defence is attack!

There is no regulation as to how you set up your players. On a couple of occasions when I played for the Hockeyroos, we played without the goalkeeper and introduced an extra field player to bolster the attack. You would do this if you really needed to score and had nothing to lose. In this set-up, you would need to win at all costs!

DEFINING GROUP GOALS

As a player in a hockey team you are both part of a group and also a member of a number of subgroups. As well, you must develop your own individual game. As a member of a team, your individual role reflects the goals and direction of the group as a whole.

John Mowat suggests that to help you plan for situations that might occur on the field, you can have your group members ask questions of themselves and answer them from various perspectives before each situation arises. Together you can answer your own questions according to the goals that the group is trying to achieve. This is a similar principle to the situation index discussed in chapter 9. As examples, he suggests the following line of questioning:

- What are we trying to achieve as a team on 16-yard hits; and within that context, what is my individual role on 16-yard hits?
- What are we trying to achieve as a group when they have the ball in the midfield; and so, for example, what is my role as a striker (subgroup) and as an individual in that situation?
- What are we trying to achieve as a group when the ball is in our attack; and within that context, what are my subgroup (striker, midfielder or defender) and individual roles in attack?
- What are we trying to achieve as a group when the ball is in our defence; and so what is my role as an individual and also a subgroup when the ball is in our defensive area?

First you should be able to answer these questions as a group (the entire team), and then as subgroups (strikers, defenders or midfielders). Finally you can determine your individual role in each situation. There is a lot to consider, so it is a good idea to think about it off the field first.

As a player on the field, you have many individual roles at one time, but the result that the group achieves is most significant. Chances are that if the group wins most of its battles and achieves its goals as a unit, then as an individual you are doing your job and will be rewarded accordingly.

When you are defending, you have three basic considerations:

1. How will you defend or implement the defensive system as a group to achieve the following goals: man-to-man marking, zone defence or a combination of the two? When you choose a method of defence, you will choose the option that best allows you to do the following:
   - Contain the ball where it is and take possession.
   - Prevent the opposition from passing or moving the ball in a manner that eliminates most defenders.
   - Recognise situations or positions of greatest danger and act to protect them.
2. How will you implement your roles as members of a subgroup? Subgroups are all over the field. As a field player you are more than likely to be a member of more than one subgroup during a match because of the quick and fluid nature of the game, but you will need to recognise and focus on each as appropriate. Such a subgroup may be the combination of two or more traditional subgroups (such as midfielders and deep defenders), which are on occasion a composite subgroup, because often their play will be interrelated.

   As a midfield subgroup, you will probably work together on the specific elements of the press by covering the dangerous central areas of the field as your first concern. As defenders, you might work on communication within your small group of players. The high strikers will have positioning objectives to achieve in the press also. You have plenty of things to work on as a subgroup, so these are examples only.

   Get together in these groups (and then as a whole team) and discuss what you are setting out to do, because the game moves quickly and any combination of players could find themselves playing together (some in an unfamiliar part of the field) to make up an important part of your subgroup. Use the system you believe will beat the opposition eventually, and have faith in it.

3. Finally, how will you play your role as an individual in this system? Within the method of defence that your team has assumed, you will need to make individual judgements regarding your tactics to counter the strengths and abilities of your direct opponent and to maximise your own strengths while protecting your weaknesses. You want to win your battles with your immediate opponent!

- In defence, position yourself so that you cannot be easily eliminated by your immediate opponent; they have the ball.
- Position yourself so that you cannot be easily eliminated if your opponent receives the ball.
- You need to make a decision according to your role as an attacker and the extent to which your opponents are involved in the play.
- If your opponent has the ball, decide where to position yourself to ensure that you can prevent that player from improving his offensive situation.
- Identify the most dangerous position for your immediate player to go to next if she receives the ball, and position yourself so as to prevent this from becoming an option.

You can make decisions before your player receives the ball according to what the opposition is likely to do and where the ball is currently located.

PLANNING YOUR DEFENCE

In the lead-up to the Olympic Games in Sydney, our group spent much time going over what we considered the basic rules for defending. You may have other rules to add, but this was the list that our group developed:

- Be composed in your defensive role.
- Be strong and low to the ground if you are making a tackle.
- In the heat of the moment, do not forget communication and calling.
- Make sure that your players cover the most dangerous lines, angles and spaces.
- Tackle on your flat stick where possible.
- Expect the unexpected when it comes to umpiring and other events.
- Play on until you hear the whistle.
- Make sure there is a balance between covering the player you are marking and covering the space that they can move into.
- Have prior knowledge of the opposition players' styles of play so that you can anticipate their attacking moves and prevent them from utilising their strengths.
- Forwards need to be quick to assume their defensive roles when required.
- Readjust your positioning according to the developments on the field.
- Contest 50/50 balls (those where both teams have an equal chance of taking clean possession) and try to win each contest.
- *Everybody* is responsible for the outcome of a defensive play because everyone has a defensive role.

THE PRESS

I refer to *the press* throughout this book. This is the way your team sets up as a group to prevent the opposition from gaining territory and penetrating from a dead-ball or a live-ball situation. You achieve this by compressing the ball into a zone on the field to make ball movement difficult for the opposition which is in possession of the ball.

The principle is that when you set up the press as a group, you look to cover the most dangerous (central) areas of the field, force the opposition players wide and hold them in that position so that it is difficult for them to generate an attacking move or to transfer the play. Most important, you prevent the direct, penetrating movement of the ball down the middle of the field towards your defensive goal.

Once the ball has been moved to an extremity of the field, your players can close the play down in that area and make it difficult for the team with the ball to transfer the play. In this situation you force the players in possession of the ball to run in a congested area, or you force them to make a low-percentage pass. In both instances, you increase the likelihood of your opponents' turning the ball over to your team.

If it is set up quickly and well, your defensive press (more attacking or defensive in its set-up as you choose) should make it difficult for the team with the ball to transfer the play from one side of the field to another without risk. If the player with the ball is allowed to make a long pass across the field, many of your players who are committed to closing the play down on one side of the field will be eliminated with that single pass. This is precisely what you are trying to prevent, and this is often where the strikers play an important defensive role.

Usually, it is the role of the high strikers to deter the cross-field pass, so these players need to be alert and ready to pounce on an interception if the attempt to change the play is made. As we've already discussed, it's also important that the players behind the high strikers call them into the correct line. Clear and early communication comes into play once again!

The strikers do need to have an instinctive feeling for when and how to close down the passing angles and lines. Communication from behind is preferable, but the speed with which the game is played prevents this from being a reality at all times. Clear and confident decision making is important for all players who will need to make instinctive decisions at times. Try to watch video of your team's set-up in these situations and improve the set-up for next time.

If you are confident of your press and your opposition has a defensive player over the ball who is known to flirt with danger, you might encourage that pass across the centre of the field and have players well positioned and ready to anticipate and capitalise on this risky pass. If the pressing players are alert and well positioned, they will make an interception in a dangerous area of the field for the team making the pass. There is a fine line between covering the line across the field with solidarity and leaving a small window of opportunity for the player with the ball to be tempted to 'thread the eye of a needle' and make the difficult pass. It is best if this play is called from the players behind who will ultimately have to make the trap, just to make sure that the key personnel are in good position to execute the critical interception. If your players are alert enough to intercept this pass, you will be in a position that allows your forwards to run at an isolated defender in deep defence or make a quick pass to another attacker who can do the same.

In a normal pressing situation, the wide high striker who is called to charge the player with the ball should run on an arc, when doing so from a wide position on the field so that he is not easily eliminated from the play and at least block the line of the dangerous pass with his body and forestick. (See figure 10.3*a*.)

If you are the wide player (left wing or right wing) and you have been called to move towards the player with the ball to apply pressure, make your first move infield and then move towards that player so that he cannot hit the ball down the middle of the field without hitting it wide of you and onto the stick of a team-mate. If you move in an arc (infield and then forward), you will have a better chance to make an interception if the ball is hit upfield. If the player chooses to hit down the middle of the field, it will need to be well wide of you, and your team-mate behind should be in good position to make the trap. Also, you will make it more difficult for the defender with the ball to eliminate you because you will be in a better, more central position to make a tackle.

You probably won't make an interception from such a close distance (the highest player in the press), but you will have done your job if you force the pass out wide or onto the stick of a team-mate. Make sure also that if you are the player pressing aggressively by running at the player with the ball, the whole pressing unit is ready for this. Usually you will not move at a player without a call from behind to do so, but obviously at times you will need to use your own judgement and make the move instinctively. (See figure 10.3a).

The overriding principle of the press is similar to what we have already discussed regarding general play: Cover the dangerous position or area first (central area of the field), force the play wide and close the play down in that position. You will know that your press is working in your attacking area when the deep defenders find it difficult to pinpoint passes to their midfield players. This will be evident if they are forced to hit the ball to a contested situation where your team has a 50/50 chance of earning possession with a good trap or tackle, or if they regularly hit the ball backwards in an effort to transfer the play. These are signals that they have limited options upfield because your press is so effective!

All players on your team can be involved in the press, and often it is the strikers who have the immediate role in this defensive play. The strikers set the tone for the press and often do the chasing, which results in the eventual turnover. This seems to be an unrewarding role at the time, but it is important for the team because it places pressure on the opposition deep defenders to make a pass when they are not prepared to do so, or it forces them to attempt to run the ball out of defence which is dangerous given the defensive area of the field that they are in. The latter is a dangerous situation for the defenders, because if as the pressing team you can apply enough pressure to turn the ball over in this position, you will be in a strong offensive position.

One way to enhance the press is by creating depth. Usually, the distance between the first line (strikers),

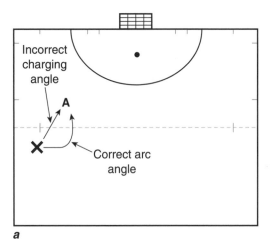

a

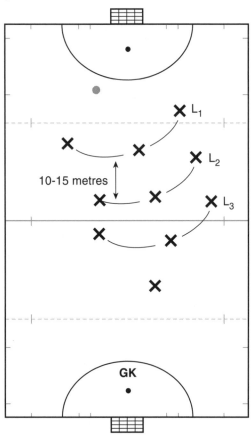

b

Figure 10.3 (a) Move in an arc. (b) Create depth between the lines.

126

the second line (midfield) and the third line (defenders) of the press is well spaced. (See figure 10.3*b*.) If the lines are too close together, one hit through a line will also eliminate the next line, and in so doing will eliminate up to seven players at one time.

If there is greater depth (10 to 15 metres [33 to 49 feet] between each line), a successful hit through the first line can still be intercepted by the second line. Also, the likelihood of this is increased because the second line has more time to react to the play and step in front of their immediate opponent to make an interception. Stagger the positioning of your players to maximise the depth of your press, but be careful not to leave too much space in between your lines for your opponents to move into as they attempt to receive the ball.

It makes sense that the role of calling the lines and the players in the press comes from the defenders and the goalkeeper, who have the best vision of the field as a whole. As discussed in chapter 9, communication in this sense is critical. Calls such as 'one step left', 'push up', 'drop back' are examples of calls that might be made by a defensive player who has vision upfield.

The defensive press can be more or less aggressive in nature according to the state of the game and the strengths and weaknesses of the opposition. If the player with the ball has a very good hard hit and therefore the ability to hit through the first line of the press, the team that is pressing might call the first line to 'fall away' and force that player to take another option that would not be her first choice. In this situation if the player attempts to hit the ball through the first line of the press, but the pressing players in that line are further from the ball as it is hit, they will have more time to react and make a trap, an interception or get a touch on the ball to change its trajectory. On the other hand, an aggressive press will not allow the player with the ball to move forward at all without a contest, but the risk is that the ball can be hit through or past the feet and stick of the running player.

63   PRESS ON FREES

Purpose

To practice setting up the press to prevent fluid movement of the ball by the opposition from all set-play situations.

Procedure

Practice free-hit situations where the press is required, such as 16-yard hits, sideline frees and defensive free hits in general play. The team with the ball tries to get it across the halfway line, and the pressing team must stop this from happening. Players need to practice calling, determine appropriate player movement for each ball movement and make sure that the most dangerous gaps are covered. This is a manufactured game situation using as much or as little of the field as necessary depending on the number of players involved. Ideally it would be a full-match replication, but you might begin by walking each scenario through as a group.

ZONE VERSUS MAN-TO-MAN

When your team is defending, you can 'zone up', play man-to-man with a spare player in deep defence acting as a sweeper or use a combination of the two. Your defensive style will probably change throughout the game according to the position of the ball on the field and the score line, so you don't have to finish the game with the defensive tactic you began with. What are you trying to achieve if your team doesn't have the ball? Simply, you will be looking to take possession from your opponents, protect your goal and give your team an opportunity to create an offensive play when you do earn possession. To do this, first the players on the team looking to take possession will make sure that the players with the ball do not get the chance to improve the position of the ball and manufacture a good offensive move.

The team with the ball could create a good offensive move by making a pass to a player in a superior position or gain territory by running with the ball upfield. The job of the defending team is to prevent this and earn possession for itself. You will make decisions about using zoning-up techniques, man-to-man marking or a combination of the two, depending on the position of the ball on the field.

Zoning Up

By preventing offensive moves by the opposition and ultimately earning possession for your team, this method of defending means that the team with the ball needs to go around the defenders or defensive unit (wide) to make an offensive move. The zone denies your opposition direct access to the critical area on the field. It is similar to a press, but it is more defensive and on a tighter scale in the defensive zone. It requires the players with the ball to move around the players in the zone rather than pressing them into a particular area.

The zone can simply be a conglomeration of players in the most dangerous defensive area. In both the press and the zone defence, the attackers are forced wide to the areas of less significant danger for the defensive team. Theoretically, the most dangerous part of the opponent's offensive areas is covered with the zone defence. Although the players are not as tightly marked as they would be in a man-to-man situation, the advantage for the defensive team is that there is little or no space for the ball to be delivered offensively without the attacking team risking a turnover or a 50/50 contest. Another advantage of the zone defence is that when the ball is turned over, the player that takes possession (now attacking, previously defending) will not be closely marked (by default) and will be in position to receive the ball without an immediate contest.

In a zone defence, the defenders cover the dangerous spaces rather than their specific opponents. They back their belief that they can protect the most dangerous area, create at least a 50/50 contest if the ball is tossed into the zone for an attacking player to move onto, or force the offensive player wide.

Just as for a zone defence in basketball, the attackers look to draw the defenders out of the defensive zone so that they can capitalise on the space created when they do so; but they may need to be patient. On the other hand, the extent to which the defending team is prepared to wait for the attackers to make an offensive move will depend largely on the score line or the context of the game. For example, if the defending team is behind on the scoreboard, they will be less patient about waiting for the attacking move to occur. Therefore, that team will need to make a calculated attempt at an interception as the attacking team moves the ball around the zone, and in so doing they risk opening up a space or giving away an offensive opportunity within the zone for the attacking team. Similarly, the attacking team may be running short on time to score, and so they have less patience for the perfect attacking opportunity and attempt to penetrate the zone with a risky pass or a low-percentage elimination skill.

Of course, if the offensive team is winning, they will be more than happy to pass the ball around the attacking circle and wait for the perfect chance to make an attacking move, or for the defensive team to leave a space that the forwards can utilise. This zone defence is best used in combination with man-to-man marking.

KEY NOTE
The team with the ball will go through a zone defence that is too wide and go around or over a zone defence that is too compact!

Players can use their body positioning to cover space on the field, and mini-zones are possible in fluid play, but usually this is in combination with man-to-man marking. An attacking team should be able to find space for a penetrating pass into the zone if it is set up too far upfield (too loose) without a combination of man-to-man marking. On the other hand, a clever overhead into an attacking pocket could eliminate the entire zone in one move if the zone is too tight.

You may devote any number of players to the defensive zone, depending on the goals and objectives and the style of play of your team. Remember that it is useful to leave some players in an outlet position to receive the ball if your team wins possession. (See figure 10.4.)

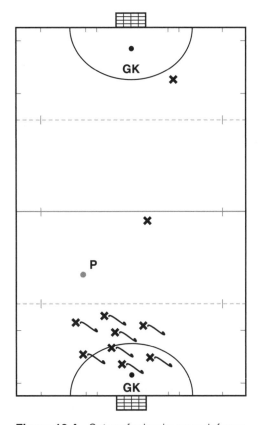

Figure 10.4 Set-up for basic zone defence.

64   ZONE DEFENCE

Purpose

To practice setting up a zone defence.

Procedure

Set up your zone defence in the circle and out to the 25-yard area by using nine defenders. Use eight attackers (including the player who will make the initial pass), and have seven of those players assisting the attack in any way they like. The attacking team tries to penetrate the zone defence. The defensive team makes it difficult for the opposition team to penetrate by forcing the attackers to pass the ball around the zone to find a penetrating space.

65   6-ON-6

Figure 10.5   6-on-6.

Purpose

For the defenders to protect the circle and outlet successfully while the attackers try to score in the normal fashion, but they must defend if the ball is turned over.

Procedure

An attacking player begins with the ball on the 50-yard line and makes a pass to another attacking player. The attackers move forward to get at goal while the defenders aggressively protect the circle. If the defenders earn possession, in order to score, one of their players must dribble over the line between the cones or pass through the cones with a push from outside the area marked with a cone at each sideline. (See figure 10.5.)

Man to Man Marking

This style of defensive play requires that the players take responsibility for an individual opponent. This is a tight marking situation that can leave the defensive team vulnerable to a penetrating pass because players, rather than the spaces, are marked. On the other hand, the direct opponent will immediately challenge the offensive player for possession on the receiving end of the pass. This defender needs to back his ability to read the play, anticipate that move and make an effective challenge at the right moment.

Space might be available for the offensive team to move into, but usually in this defensive mode there is a spare player in deep defence to clean up the spillage after a challenge for possession. This player will not have a player to mark as such; rather, his role is to read the play, call the play, make interceptions and tidy up if a ball spills loose.

The spare defensive player (the sweeper) is in good position to call the other defensive players into line or into better position to mark closely his immediate player, because he will not be distracted by the movement of an immediate opponent. That is not to say that such an opponent will not arrive on the scene, but the sweeper (initially without the responsibility of an immediate opponent) is in good position to pick up the spare player in the attacking circle. Another defensive player might then assume the sweeping role. In most instances the sweeper marks the dangerous space in the centre of the circle taking the line from the player in possession to the goal, or if the ball is further upfield, the sweeper marks the more central and dangerous position on the field. When you are marking man-to-man, get goal side and inside your player.

The principle of marking man to man is that your positioning usually requires you to be on the defensive goal side of your immediate opponent and inside the field relative to that player's positioning. This means that you will be positioned between your defensive goal (the attacker's goal) and your opponent, while at the same time positioning yourself so that your opponent is closer to the sideline than you are—you are 'goal side and inside' your opponent. (See figure 10.6.) You also have good vision of the ball as it approaches and the player you are marking simultaneously.

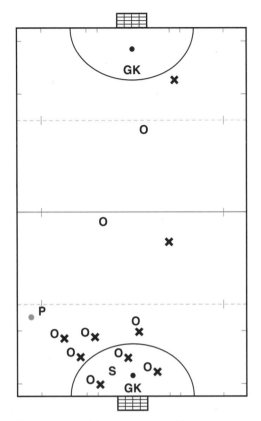

Figure 10.6 Man-to-man marking.

The other option is to mark from in front of your opposition player. With the introduction of the 'no off side' rule, this is an increasingly common marking alternative. You can mark 50 to 60 metres (about 55 to 66 yards) in front of your opponent in the right situation, which means that you are not eliminated from attacking opportunities, but you will rely heavily on the players behind you to call your line.

66   MAN-TO-MAN IN THE CIRCLE

Purpose
To practice marking closely while the attackers practice leading in this situation and the player with the ball practices delivering the ball to a tightly marked player.

Procedure
Have two or more attackers and defenders in the circle. The defenders practice marking tightly (with body or stick contact), and the attackers lead for the ball. The player with the ball must connect with one of the attackers, who receives then shoots at goal or wins a penalty corner. Increase the competitiveness of the drill by counting the successful goal shots or penalty corners awarded versus the successful interceptions or blocks made by the defenders. You can practice marking in any drill during a training session.

HOLDING POSSESSION

You and your team need to practice this skill, just as you need to recognise appropriate occasions to use it. Many times in a game situation it will be sensible for your team to hold possession without necessarily creating attacking moves. You can do this in any position on the field, depending on your reason for holding possession. Obviously, the defensive area is not ideal for holding possession for extended periods. If you make an error, the punishment by the opposition forwards can be great. But in the midfield you can pass back to the deep defenders to stretch the opposition forwards and make them chase the ball.

67　KEEPING OFF

Purpose

To practice the skill of holding possession in a contested environment.

Procedure

In a small-game situation in a confined area, each team attempts to make three, four or five consecutive passes (start with a small number and work towards making more passes as you get better) without necessarily moving forward. Once a team makes those consecutive passes, the team is awarded a point and begins the task again. If the ball is turned over, the other team tries to do the same thing.

68　HOLDING THE BALL ON YOUR STICK

Purpose

To practice holding the ball in your possession for situations that don't allow you to make a pass.

Procedure

Set up a small area (3 metres by 3 metres [9 feet by 9 feet]) and take turns with another player to hold the ball in your possession. You can move in the area, but you must not let your opponent steal the ball.

69　DOUBLE POSSESSION

Purpose

To practice passing the ball and holding onto the ball with the support of only one other player in a confined area such as the attacking pocket of the field. This situation might occur if you are running the clock down because your team is ahead on the scoreboard and there is very little time left on the clock.

Procedure

In the confined area (5 metres by 5 metres [16 feet by 16 feet]), hold the ball and pass to another player when necessary so that two players keep the ball off a single defender. This skill is best performed in the attacking right pocket of the field so that your back is not to the attacking circle and you can make a quick pass into the circle if necessary. It is a good time-wasting technique, as is the previous drill.

The following are situations in which you might want to consider holding possession without necessarily generating offensive moves:

• Your team is not executing the basic skills with precision, and simple passing can bring the players' focus back to the basic skills of the game.

• There is very little time left on the clock and your team is winning. You want to make sure that you don't turn the ball over and give your opponent an opportunity to even the score or to get ahead. Be careful not to do this prematurely. But if you have only two or three minutes to go and your team is one or two goals ahead, find your best ball handlers who can pass between themselves and hold possession in the attacking right-hand corner of the field.

• You have the ball in a breakaway situation, but the situation looking forward is not conducive to a solo attacking move. In this situation you might slow down and wait for fellow attackers and midfielders to catch up with you and provide support. You will need to hold possession without necessarily moving forward quickly.

• The best part of the field in which to do this is the right attacking pocket. Not only is this a long distance from your opponent's goal, but you also make it difficult for the opposition players to steal the ball because you are protected by the sideline and the backline. Be careful not to obstruct, and if the opponents do get a touch, make sure they only knock it out of bounds. When only seconds are left on the clock, it is easier to cross the ball into the circle from the right side to jag a last-minute penalty corner or a goal shot.

• At designated times in the game you may want to sacrifice your attacking potential and make the opposition chase the ball with the aim of wearing out your opponents. It is tiring to chase the ball, and if you hold possession effectively by passing the ball around, you will tire the opposition. If they want to dispossess you, they will have to press and chase, particularly if you are passing freely over long distances. When your opposition has been chasing the ball for a couple of minutes, you can create attacking moves with greater ease. The midfielders and opposition forwards will be less able to chase and make effective tackles because they are physically tired. It is usually more tiring to chase the ball around the field and hunt possession than it is to hold possession as a group.

Be aware of the time remaining on the clock. You will need to know where the clock is on the field and whether it is functioning. This is not necessarily an obvious point, because many players simply play the same game regardless of the time left on the clock. This is part of the idea of taking responsibility for what happens on the field as individuals and as leaders.

If you cannot see a functioning clock, ask the umpire how much time remains so that you can make an informed decision about pulling back on the attacking front. Make sure you hold possession at an appropriate time. Beware the temptation to run the clock down too early, but be sure to use this tactic when appropriate.

There are no hard-and-fast rules about setting up your team on the field and deciding on the way you'll play, but it makes sense to capitalise on your team's strengths and to punish your opposition's weaknesses while protecting your own weaknesses. Be flexible and react to changes as they occur during the game regarding the score line, the match conditions, the style and form of your opposition and particular players within the team.

The fundamental choices that you have revolve around the extent to which your team attacks and defends. There are no absolutes when it comes to playing styles, but you also need to consider marking techniques (often a combination), the set-up of your press, playing resources devoted to all-out attack and defence, when and how to hold possession and the individual roles that players have within the team according to the objectives of the team as a whole in each particular situation. There is a lot to think about, but with enough planning and practice you can do it all!

CHAPTER 11

BREAKAWAYS AND COUNTERATTACKS

Because good attacking opportunities don't necessarily come along very often, you must make the most of them, just as you need to prevent the opposition from taking advantage of its offensive opportunities. This chapter looks at the implementation and defence of some of the best possible attacking scenarios: breakaways and counterattacks.

Well-executed counterattacks and breakaways can be rewarding scoring opportunities if you are ready and able to execute them. But whether you are attacking or defending in this situation, speed of movement and quick team transition are the key.

No matter how much a team seems to defend, there is often an opportunity to attack—even against the run of play. This could well come about from a counterattacking opportunity, as long as you are ready to make the most of the chance when it presents itself. Always be ready to attack!

But teams sometimes become so intent on all-out attack that they become vulnerable to the counterattack. This occurs when the attacking team commits numbers to the attacking play, then loses possession and is outnumbered in defence. The opposition team now in possession breaks into attack against the run of play. This can occur as a result of a penalty corner which turns the possession to the defensive team, or any other defensive play which turns quickly to attack in favour of the team that has been defending. The team that has lost possession in this play and has overcommitted to that offensive effort is now outnumbered in its defence, so the players must quickly get back to defend.

Have a game plan for situations where your team is counterattacking or breaking, as well as defending these situations. Have a balance (which will be reflected in the style of play that your team has chosen) between offensive and defensive priorities. This allows you to make the most of your chances by providing support to your forwards while also adequately defending your goal.

135

Speed is key to a well-executed breakaway.

BREAKING AND THE COUNTERATTACK

Breakaways are a significant component of a counterattacking situation, and they can occur in other situations as well. They don't necessarily begin in the defensive zone, but they require that there be significant attacking space to move into with speed. This may come about because of a defensive deficit on the other team, who has focused on attacking plays, or because a forward has eliminated one of the deepest defensive players and is running quickly towards goal and an isolated defender.

The key to making the most of a counterattacking opportunity is speed. Speed in transition will ensure that the attacking play can make the most of the opposition's vulnerability because of their lack of numbers in defence, and your forwards can isolate the few defenders who are in defensive position. Penalty-corner defence can quickly turn to an attacking opportunity in this way. The forwards on the team defending the penalty corner (all players who are not involved on the defensive circle) can set up so that they are in good position to counter quickly if the opportunity arises. In this situation your team might choose to have two players high up the field near the attacking 25-yard line, one high striker in the attacking circle and two players wide on the halfway line.

Usually two or three players will be on the opposition team who are covering the central area of the field (the most dangerous area), so a pass made quickly and wide to a player on the halfway line can be made further upfield with a minimum of fuss. In this situation, the ball can move from the defensive circle (where it is turned over) to the attacking circle with two or three crisp passes. As is the case in most attacking and defensive scenarios, the basic passing skills will determine the success of this counterattacking play.

As we discussed in a previous chapter, the ball will travel more quickly with a pass than by individuals dribbling the ball upfield; so in the interest of breaking quickly and making the most of your greater numbers in attack, pinpoint attackers with a firm pass upfield rather than running the ball out of defence. This will require you to know your passing options before receiving the ball, just as we have discussed in earlier chapters. The difficult skill is in making yourself aware of the option early.

Your defender might gain possession and pinpoint a pass to a high striker against the run of play. If you are that attacking player, take responsibility and make your position known to your team-mates early or before the turnover occurs; as a defender be sure to glance up the field when you have a chance to make yourself aware of counterattacking opportunities, should you earn possession. You will do this many times in a game without the occasion to make the pass. But on the occasion that it becomes an available option, you need to be ready and have the awareness to use it.

Be direct with your attack. If there is an opportunity to move the ball up the centre of the field rather than move the ball wide as a first option, do so because you will get the ball into the offensive area more quickly than if you go wide. The opposition players now trying to defend their goal will run hard to get back into a cover position, so the team with the ball should try to make a good attacking move before their opponents get back into defensive position.

If one of your forwards breaks in the midfield or further upfield, make sure there are players who run hard to get up in support. Be careful that you don't suffer the same fate as your opposition by overcommitting too many players to the attacking move; but there should be players running to support in attack every bit as hard as the defending team is running to get back in defence.

If someone gets up in support of the ball carrier, it will at the very least create indecision in the minds of the defenders by providing passing options for the player with the ball. So even if you make the effort to get there in support and don't receive a pass, your effort will not be wasted.

REACTING TO THEIR COUNTERATTACK

When your opposition breaks and your defenders are outnumbered, you will need to minimise the attacking possibilities for that team. Obviously, it will not be your intention to allow this situation to occur, but you can be certain that it will happen at some time. Some principles to follow in this situation include making sure that you cover the most dangerous area first, delay the play and push or channel the attackers wide.

I have already mentioned that the most dangerous area of the field is the centre corridor, and as an attacker you will try to move through this area. When your team is defending, try to cover this central area before worrying about the players who are positioned in a wider position. Get numbers into this central area as quickly as possible and force the attacking team to go around you. This will slow the attacking play and allow your players to get back in defence simultaneously.

If you are isolated as a defender and have an attacking player running at you with speed, don't commit to a tackle unless you are 100 percent certain that you will win possession. If you do attempt to make a tackle and get eliminated in the process, there is very little or no backup and the attacker will be able to run quickly at the isolated goalkeeper. The best thing you can do is to delay the ball carrier by remaining between him and the goal and try to force that player into a wide position while giving your team-mates a good opportunity to get back in cover defence.

You will need to do more than just get numbers back in defence to hinder the counter-attacking team, but this is a priority. Someone needs to take responsibility for calling the line of each player as he sets up in his defensive position. The goalkeeper is usually the deepest player and therefore will have the clearest view and the best perspective of how the action is taking place. So as discussed in chapter 8, this player needs to take control and call the defenders into the best position. The goalkeeper should not be the only player calling the play, because all players should communicate their intentions and give directions for other players when appropriate.

When I refer to the relevant players in each situation as 'defenders' or 'attackers', it is not necessarily the players who lined up at the beginning of the match in a defensive role that would be best placed to act in a defensive or attacking role. It might be that midfielders or even strikers find themselves best positioned to get back and play the role of a defender until the traditional defenders who are momentarily out of position can catch up and get back in position. Similarly, the player who lined up as a defender might be best placed to take an attacking opportunity by overlapping into the attacking region.

On occasion you'll find that offensive players have the opportunity to chase back in defence, but they don't do so because they think it is not in their job description. Forget this attitude. If, as a forward, you are best positioned to get back and help, do so without a second thought. If it turns out that too many players are assuming a defensive role, you can drop out of the play and provide a useful outlet for when your team recovers possession, but you can't necessarily catch up with the play if numbers are short. Act first, then react to your decision as the play develops.

The last resort for a team outnumbered in defence is to commit a 'professional' foul, as we touched on briefly in chapter 5. This is a tactic using a low-grade foul such as a clumsy tackle or messy footwork to stop the ball or the player and to give a free hit away to delay the play and give the defensive players an opportunity to get numbers back into cover position. If you can do this, you will give other players in your team the opportunity to get back into position. Some players make an art of this skill, but be careful not to make it a regular feature of your game and earn a yellow or red card, which will see you spending time in the sin bin. Choose your moment carefully, do it safely and exhaust all other options before committing a professional foul!

70   COUNTER FROM DEEP DEFENCE

Purpose

To practice executing breakaway situations in attack and defence over a long distance.

Procedure

Set up the attacking team with one player over the ball at the top of the defensive circle (player A), one player wide on each end of the 50-yard line (players B and C), and one player wide on each side of the 25-yard line (players D and E). The defensive team has its deepest defender on the 25-yard line (player X_1) and another two defenders on the 50-yard line (players X_2 and X_3). Player A passes the ball crisply to player B or C (attackers). Those players try to find their high players (D or E) with a sharp pass. Meanwhile, players X_1, X_2 and X_3 determine who should go to the ball carrier (this will depend on how quickly the ball is moved by the attackers) to delay the play. The others get into cover defence as quickly as possible to provide support. The goalkeeper calls the play and defends the circle according to the approaching play. (See figure 11.1.)

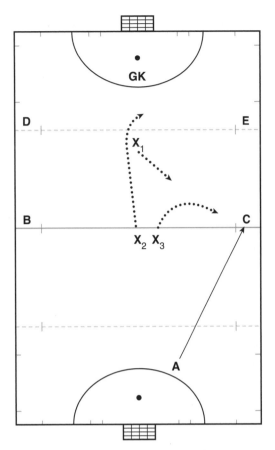

Figure 11.1 Counter from deep defence.

71   BREAKAWAY IN ATTACK

Purpose

To break close to the circle and capitalise on the isolated defender.

Procedure

Player A passes the ball to player B, who breaks into the attacking 25-yard area. Player C confronts player B to delay until player A gets back in cover defence or otherwise makes a clean tackle. If a clean tackle is not possible, then delay the play. Player C should try to confront player B outside the 25-yard area in the case of an untidy foul, which would otherwise earn the attacking team a penalty corner. Player B tries to get into that 25-yard zone and the circle as quickly as possible to shoot or make a pass to player D. Do this from the right, left and centre of the field. The goalkeeper calls the play and reacts according to the play. (See figure 11.2.)

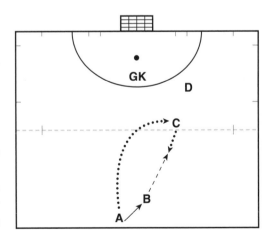

Figure 11.2 Breakaway in attack.

139

72 DECISION MAKING IN BREAKAWAY SITUATIONS

Purpose

To practice recognising and reacting to breakaway situations offensively and defensively.

Procedure

Two independent games of 4 x 4 are played across the field, one in each 25 yard zone. Each of the ends is also a composite team (team A and team B, each with eight players) ready to attack or defend as a unit as per the instructions of the coach. While the small 4 x 4 games are going on, the coach designates a team to attack the other end in which situation that team (A or B) tries to score and the other composite team tries to dispossess that team and score at the other end. Each team keeps its 4 x 4 score and each end keeps its score. The winning team has the best 4 x 4 score and end score. (See figure 11.3.)

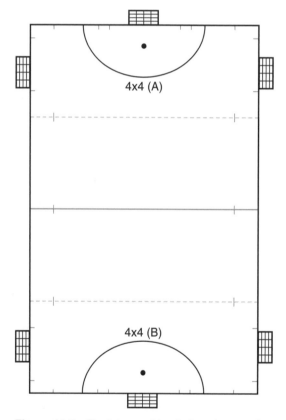

Figure 11.3 Decision making in breakaway situations.

73   INTERCEPT AND COUNTER

Purpose

To practice being alert to make an interception and then quickly counterattack when possible. Encourage the intercepting players to get high so that when the ball is turned over, the defenders can be eliminated with a crisp pass rather than allowing the other team to get back into the play because the attackers are dribbling the ball—a slower method of moving the ball.

Procedure

Player A tries to pass to player B or C, each of whom is at one end of an intercept box marked by the cones. Players B and C can only lead laterally, so they can't lead towards the ball. Players D and E try to make an intercept using player F to call their positional lines according to the lateral movements of players B and C. If players D and E make an intercept they make a quick counterattack towards the goal and player F can move to support the attack while players B and C chase to defend. Player A and the goalkeeper need to communicate clearly regarding the defensive effort in this situation. (See figure 11.4.)

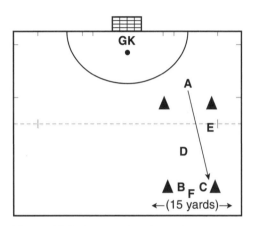

Figure 11.4   Intercept and counter.

Breakaway situations can be very damaging if they are executed with precision and planning. Make sure that you break or counter with speed, and be aware of the passing options before the play begins—this should be a natural part of your game by now! To maximise the speed of your new attacking situation, pass the ball rather than run with it if there is an alternative. Punish and eliminate isolated defenders quickly using your superior numbers if you can, and get to the attacking circle before the opposition gets there to break your attacking play down or nullify your numeric advantage.

When defending, cover the most dangerous central area first and then worry about other passing options. If you are the isolated defender, be careful not to get eliminated before you have support from other team-mates. Delay the play if you can—drop away with the play but avoid being eliminated quickly at all costs. If you can delay the play and force it wide to a less direct and dangerous attacking area, then you will have done a great job. By delaying the play, your team-mates will catch up and get numbers into defence to back you and your goalkeeper up.

CHAPTER 12

SET PLAYS

Slick and confident set-play execution is an important element of the game of hockey. Some teams do all they can to implement set plays, and they spend many hours each week practicing their execution. Slick application of set-play skills can win games, and sloppy defence of them can lose games for you. So pay particular attention to your preparation for set plays.

You probably think of set plays as attacking moves such as penalty corners, free hits outside the circle and in general play. In many cases they are offensive in nature, but set plays will also get you out of defensive trouble. Defensive outlets (getting the ball safely out of defence) and defensive penalty-corner moves, a particularly important and complicated set play (see chapter 13), are also possibilities that can benefit your team and turn defence into attack very quickly. If you build these rehearsed pieces into your training regimen, you will gradually feel more comfortable introducing them into the game situation, and you will be well on your way to moulding your team into a professional outfit!

FREE HITS OUTSIDE THE ATTACKING CIRCLE

These offensive situations are set plays that your team can rehearse and execute with precision to create a good attacking option. Although you would ultimately like to score, you will usually get a good result to convert a long corner or a free hit outside the circle into a penalty corner or a goal shot, and your team can develop any number of combinations to make this happen.

First be aware of the extent to which your opponents are set up defensively. If you have players in the attacking circle who are clearly unmarked or would be in position to isolate a lone defender if they had the ball, then the free hit should be passed to that player with urgency. Often, however, the defenders are well set up so as to make these early options unavailable. This is an opportunity to execute the other set-play moves that you practice away from the game situation.

Usually you will look to stretch the defensive unit wide in an effort to create space for your forwards to move into. Maintain some width in your attacking structure, but move so that you receive the ball in a strong attacking (central) position at the end of the play. Similarly, if you are the defending team, you will look to remain compact in your set-up to protect the most dangerous area of the circle or field first, and in so doing force the attackers to receive the ball in a wide (less dangerous) position for the defenders.

Your team may have a hierarchy of outcomes for attacking moves. In this way it may be your intention to do the following:

1. Set up a goal shot.
2. Win a penalty corner.
3. Win a free hit closer to the centre of the goal or field or in a better position offensively.

Once you have determined that you will gain no advantage by getting the ball moving quickly, take your time to set up these plays, making sure that each player understands her role. Each play will be different according to the position around the circle in which the free hit is taken.

Here are some tips for set plays inside the attacking zone or attacking 25-yard area:

- Make sure the skill execution of all the players is of a very high standard.
- Take your time in the heat of the moment to get the skill execution right.
- Have purpose in your movement and leading when you don't have the ball.
- Don't force a pass that is not 'on'.
- Have variety in the plays you use.

The general principle in this situation is to create space for your attacking players to receive the ball. You achieve this through the movement of the attackers within the circle, which will stretch the defenders away from the critical scoring area directly in front of the goal.

When attackers move defenders around in the circle, space opens up for the ball to be passed into the circle for a deflection, another type of goal shot, or a penalty corner. Players can also play the role of screens, which block the sight of defenders and allow the ball to travel through to the deeper forwards. The following are some possible scenarios.

Scenario 1a

Player B receives the ball at the top of the circle from player C. In this move, attacker C might lead out of the area (calling for the ball), while attacker A moves into that area, receives the ball and plays according to the team's hierarchy of options:

1. Receive and have a shot at goal.
2. Receive the ball and win a penalty corner.
3. Bunt the ball back to player A or another attacking player to move in and have a shot on goal or win a penalty corner.

The timing of these leads needs to be coordinated, and you can introduce a dummy pass to create further confusion for the defenders. Remember to communicate this play to the relevant attackers in the lead-up.

Scenario 1b

Player A would stand over the ball as though to take the 'free', then dummy a hit or a push pass in one direction before moving away from the ball for player B to move in and make a pass in another direction. In this time, if the dummy is convincing, the defenders should be all but entirely committed to the dummy pass, and the forwards can take position accordingly, ready for the real play. (See figure 12.1a-b.)

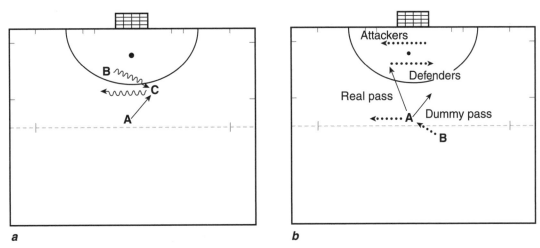

a   b

Figure 12.1 (a) Player C makes space for player B who ends up receiving the ball. (b) Player A sells the dummy right (the defenders react to this) and player B makes the pass to an attacker.

Scenario 2

Widen the goal. This simple set play can always be set up no matter what variation has been chosen around the attacking circle. In this particular instance, always have an attacking player just outside the line of each goalpost (players A and B). This will ensure that a player is always there to 'widen' the goal. Also, these two players can time their leads to cross over so as to confuse the players who are marking them, and they can make sure the goalkeeper and deep defenders are unsighted as the free hit is taken.

Both these players would move so as to end up in a position to make a deflection close to the goal with the ball arriving from any angle, which gives the goalkeeper very little time to react, as previously discussed. (See figure 12.2.)

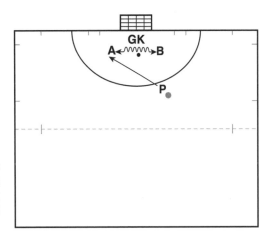

Figure 12.2 Players A and B begin outside the line of the goalposts and dart to the other side to confuse the defenders and block the sight of the goal keeper. They are there to make deflections and widen the goal for the attacking team.

145

Scenario 3

Use players in the circle as screens so that the defenders are blinded momentarily. These screen players (players A and B) can dummy (fake) over the ball as they lead, or they can remain stationary, as though to make a trap. The defender will be unsighted momentarily, and the ball can travel through the congested area of the circle to another attacking player. (See figure 12.3.)

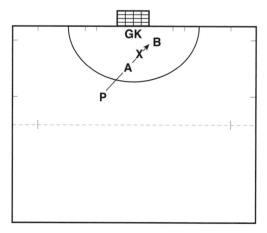

Figure 12.3 Players A and B block the vision of the defender (player C) momentarily and play over the ball as though to make a trap. The ball travels through the congested area of the field to attackers in a better offensive position.

FREE HITS IN GENERAL PLAY

It seems obvious, but these free hits are also set plays. It is only because these plays are so frequent that we don't always recognise that their execution is often planned.

First, make sure you get the ball back into play as quickly as possible to give your team the best chance of catching the opposition out of position. While you move to collect the ball, you can scan the play ahead to determine the possible passing options for when you are ready to take the free hit. You will also determine the urgency required so that once you have the ball, you can simply concentrate on making the pass as quickly as you deem necessary. In other instances you may want to slow the play down to allow your players to set up in good position offensively and defensively, according to the position of the ball. Or you may want to run the clock down when your team is ahead towards the end of a half or the game.

Set plays in general play differ according to their position on the field. For instance, frees in your defensive area will be of a more conservative nature than in attack. (See figure 2.11 for relative safety and danger areas of the field in chapter 2.) These may be good opportunities for you to transfer or switch the play from one side of the field to another or to work the ball up the sideline using tight 2-on-1s until a good attacking opportunity presents itself. (See chapter 6 for explanations and drills for 2-on-1s.) Make sure that with every free taken, you place your team in a better position.

DEFENSIVE OUTLETS

The most important thing in this area is to create several low-risk options for the player over the ball to get it moving out of defence. The movement of the ball when coming out of defence will require manipulation of the opposition press to create spaces to deliver the ball to your players. Players in the midfield need to make leads and remember to reload to create useful spaces and offensive opportunities for the player with the ball. (See chapter 10 for information about the press.) Be patient, and the spaces will eventually open up!

The following is a hierarchy of options for the static outlet:

1. Quickly look for an opportunity to find a spare player with a penetrating pass high in attack.

2. Look for a spare player in midfield.

3. If both these options are unavailable, switch the play or make a short pass that changes the static situation to one that is dynamic or fluid. The pressing team will need to react to this, and space will open up for your players to move into and for the player with the ball to make a pass.

Set up your play with options on either side of the ball. If the ball is in the middle of the pitch, then a wide option on either side is ideal. Have players (usually the midfielders) ahead of the ball moving to create space to receive. These are the players you may want to get the ball to, so they need to lead laterally behind the opposition's press in order to receive the ball.

If you're near the sideline, then you may need a back-pass option in order to open up and change the play. An overhead is also a useful way of clearing a congested sideline area. Another method of changing the lines of the opposition press is the 'touch and go' technique between two players over the ball. But remember that the ball must move at least one metre in a dead-ball situation. Although the ball doesn't travel far, it enables the player that receives the pass to track with the ball on an angle to open up different passing angles.

This short pass from a static or dead-ball situation also will serve the purpose of getting your opponents moving towards the player with the ball, which can create space for you upfield. If they don't move forward, you can continue moving with the ball. Try to break the lines of the press by getting the ball in behind these players. Do this by hitting the ball past the feet of the approaching player into space further up the field. If the closest player does not approach the ball carrier, you can move forward and hit the ball past the feet of that player. If the pressing player drops away, you can continue to move forward and look for a pass in the new or changed environment.

If your team has the ball on a free hit in defence, you will look to get the ball quickly to a player that is free while high in attack or in the midfield. The preferred option is to find a loose attacking player upfield with one penetrating pass, but this is unlikely to be an available option because the opposition team will set up a defensive press to eliminate this possibility as a first priority. Look for this prospect, but don't force it if there is a high chance of a turnover. You can develop a hierarchy of options for this part of the game also.

If neither of these options is available early, the opposition has probably set up a good press to keep the ball in their attacking region. As a defender taking the free hit in a static situation such as a 16-yard hit, you need to make a pass which changes the lines of this press. Once the ball is 'live', the attacking team will react to this, and gaps might appear in the midfield or further upfield.

If there is not a good attacking option upfield, a lateral pass is a good option. Remember that this is a dangerous area of the field in which to turn the ball over, so make your lateral-outlet pass a safe one. A lateral pass to a wing halfback or another deep defender can be enough to change the line and positioning of the opposition team so that your midfielders can work themselves into an unmarked position to receive the ball in the second or third play.

When defending the circle in free-hit situations, you want to congest the critical scoring area and prevent the attacking team getting to the circle. But if they do get into the circle you want to force any shot that is taken to be from a wide position in the circle—that is, the exact opposite of what you are trying to achieve in attack. By not overreacting to attackers' movements, but simply covering the appropriate lines, you protect the central area where goal shots are most effective. One defensive player should be directly in the line of the free hit and the goal. The sole job of this player is to make a trap.

A combination of zone defence and man-to-man marking could be employed in these situations, as discussed in chapter 10. Attackers in critical scoring areas should be marked tightly with other defenders offering cover and limiting offensive passing options in the area.

74   SWITCHING THE PLAY

Purpose

To become confident to make a lateral pass which switches the play so a midfield lead or an attacker's lead can be satisfied on the second and third play. These receiving players also practice timing their leads according to the play.

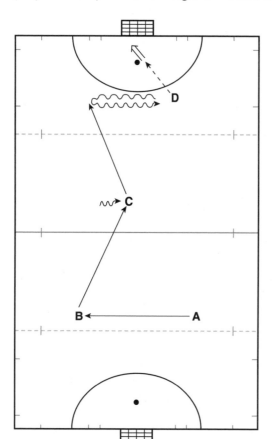

Procedure

Set up a free-hit situation whereby player A looks upfield and then makes a lateral pass across the field to player B. Player B passes to player C who is leading and then passes upfield to player D, who leads, receives in a central position and then shoots at goal. (See figure 12.4.)

Figure 12.4 Switching the play.

75 PRESS AND OUTLET PRACTICE

Purpose

To practice setting up the defensive press while the team with the ball tries to get the ball out by manipulating the press.

Procedure

Using full-team set-ups if possible, take the free hit at the defensive 25-yard line and look to get the ball upfield as quickly and effectively as possible. The pressing team must prevent this and fight for possession.

PENALTY STROKES

This is a relatively closed skill because no external variables can interrupt your skill execution. The only variable affecting your ability to execute the skill will be your attitude to the task. This is usually the case with all the skills of the game, so remember that overnight you will not lose your ability to execute a skill that you have developed. Believe in your ability, and in a match situation do what you have done in practice a thousand times.

The players who are best at taking penalty strokes appear to be confident in their technique, and they decide very early (perhaps before the game according to the relative strengths and weaknesses of the goalkeeper) where they will place the ball. It's likely that they also have at least two good options (one to each side) so that the goalkeeper has difficulty anticipating where the ball will be fired.

- The technique is much the same as for a push pass, except that you may want to elevate the ball more than in general play by angling your stick so that the top edge is behind the bottom edge. Keep your eyes over the ball and transfer your weight and the face of the stick towards the target in the follow-through. (See figure 12.5a-c.)

Figure 12.5 (a) Starting position. (b) Eyes over the ball, transfer your weight towards your target. (c) Keep your stick on the ball for as long as possible.

- Before beginning the penalty stroke, you must be behind and within playing distance of the ball and you cannot use a 'dragging action' like you would for a drag flick on a penalty corner.
- Make sure the face of your stick is facing your target when the ball leaves your stick.

Whatever your technique (within the rules), develop a consistent routine when you practice. Remember that, as is the case when shooting for goal in 'live' play, placement of the ball can be more important than the generation of power. Unless the ball is moving at goal, there is no chance of scoring. At the very least, force the goalkeeper to need to make a great save!

Set plays are important components of the game. They are attacking and defensive in nature, so they can create scoring opportunities as well as get your team out of trouble. To get the critical timing and combinations right, practice these plays at training with the players in the group who will play together in game situations. Good teamwork is important here, as is the execution of the basic skills of the game.

When taking free hits, look for the most attacking or penetrating option first, and then be more conservative as necessary to get the ball moving in a live situation. For example, if you have the ball on a 16-yard hit and several options are available, use the most aggressive attacking option, which is usually the most penetrating pass. But be careful to respect the relative dangers of the particular parts of the field. As a last resort (but perhaps a safe one), choose a non-penetrating pass, which will keep possession for your team and open up other offensive opportunities in the next play.

□ CHAPTER 13 □

PENALTY CORNERS

Penalty corners in attack and defence are some of the most obvious of all the set play alternatives. Many skills and movements required for set plays are relevant only for penalty corner execution. Penalty corners and your team's execution of them in attack and defence can make all the difference for your team on the scoreboard. They provide an excellent opportunity to score if you have players on the team with reliable specialist skills. A solid and reliable corner defence is worth its weight in gold too. Devote significant time and effort to thinking through and practicing your penalty corners at both ends of the field, according to the particular opposition you are facing and your team's strengths in this area. In attack, use traditional plays as well as some imagination for rebounds, passes, deflections and signals to create scoring opportunities, and plan the use of your personnel for penalty corner attacks and defence.

ATTACKING PENALTY CORNERS

Attacking penalty corners present a good opportunity to score, and you can plan for their precise execution before the game and according to the particular opposition. Make sure your penalty-corner combination practices together often and that each player works hard at getting his contribution right. Time spent on technique development for penalty-corner skills will ensure that you get a good result for this offensive move.

   Your team might develop as many as 50 different attacking penalty-corner variations with the ball pushed into the field from the left or the right of the circle (as you look at it from the circle top), but it is likely you will only use a handful on a regular basis. You will increase your repertoire as you attempt to outsmart specific opponents by taking into consideration their various defensive strengths and weaknesses in combination with your attacking strengths. The premise is to keep your variations as simple as possible. The fewer moves involved in the variation, the simpler the execution and the lower the likelihood of error and wasted scoring opportunity.

The basic components of all attacking penalty corners are very similar in nature, so work hard to develop the basic skills such as pushing the ball into play, trapping and hitting at goal. If your team gets these elements right, then you will create opportunities to use your more complicated variations that develop from this solid foundation. Also, in most situations you will have two or more field players in defence (covering the central area of the field) plus the goalkeeper as shown in figure 13.1.

The push-out and the trap components provide the foundation of almost every penalty-corner variation. Get these components right, and you will give your team the best possible chance to convert attacking opportunities.

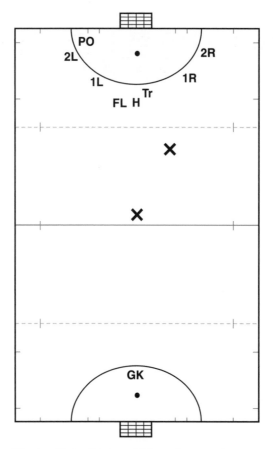

Figure 13.1 Basic positions for penalty corners.

The Push-Out

This seems a relatively simple, closed skill because very few physical variables can interfere with the execution. However, it is one of the most critical skills because it brings the ball into play and gives your team a chance to get the rest of the variation right. It is a thankless task because very rarely will you get direct recognition for a good push-out, but when you make a mistake you will certainly hear about it!

Once you have pushed the ball infield, your job is not done! Your next role is to make good position to pounce on a rebound or receive a pass for a deflection or to make another pass to a team-mate. Similarly, your role might be to lead and call for the ball as if to receive a pass, and in so doing distract the defenders. The ability to implement all of these roles for the 'pusher-outer' is important when it comes to maximising the outcome of the penalty corner. Slick execution of this skill sets the tone for the rest of the variation. You need to be able to disguise the direction of the push-out according to the selected variation.

The push-out is not the traditional 'push' pushing technique that you would use in general play. The ball has to stay in the crook of the stick, and the stick face is pointing down towards the ground for as long as possible. It is more of a drag from behind than the typical pushing technique.

Kate Starre, two-time Olympic gold medallist with the Hockeyroos and now a coach in the United States, is a player who was excellent at the push-out in these plays. She outlines the following tips for pushing the ball into play on the left side of the goal:

- Ensure that your right foot is behind the line.
- Line your feet up so that if you were to draw a line from one foot to the other, it would point in the direction of the trapper (your target).
- Position your feet more than shoulder-width apart and get into a squat position. Get low and make sure your weight is on the back foot.
- Both arms are straight (the left may be slightly bent) with the ball in the crook of the stick. The ball should be about a foot in front of your body.
- The stick is parallel with your feet and fairly low to the ground.
- From the starting position, slowly move the ball forward in the crook of the stick. The initial movement doesn't have to be quick. Keep the ball in the crook of the stick and pull the stick through in a straight line towards your target.
- Increase the stick speed as you get the ball moving, but keep the ball on your stick for as long as possible.
- Transfer your weight from your back foot to your front foot to maximise the power you can generate.
- Use a little rotation through the hips at the end of the pull for extra power.
- Keep your head down throughout the action.
- Move into position for rebounds and the next play. (See figure 13.2*a-d*.)

KEY NOTE
So often you will see players push the ball into play and admire their handiwork, then relax and watch the ensuing play. If you are in the attacking circle, always be ready for the ball to come your way, even if you think you have done your job!

Kate Starre, one of the best-ever executors of the penalty-corner push-out, demonstrates this skill at the Sydney 2000 Olympic Games.

Figure 13.2 (*a*) Line your feet up with your target. (*b*) Get low, have the ball in the crook of the stick and transfer your weight from your back foot (behind the line) to your front foot towards your target, keeping your eyes on the ball all the way. (*c*) Drag the ball in the crook of your stick towards the target with your weight now on your front foot. (*d*) Follow through towards the target.

76   PUSH-OUT REPETITION

Purpose

To become comfortable with the pushing technique and to achieve accuracy and speed.

Procedure

Repetition is the only way to get better at the push-out. At the top of the circle set up a target (using cones or a car tyre) that represents the trapper. In sets of five, aim for the target. Count the number of hits, rest, and then try again. Once you have the accuracy, have someone time how long it takes for the ball to leave your stick and hit the target. If you have access to a speed gun, use that to measure the speed of your push-out. The idea is to be accurate and powerful and to push the ball flat along the ground.

You can push the ball from the right of the circle too (as the attacking team looks at goal from the circle top). You might choose to do this if the conditions of the surface cause the ball to bounce out from the left or if you think your opposition has a particular defensive weakness that is vulnerable to this alternative tactic. It is more difficult to generate the same power from this side. Kate Starre outlines the following key points for the push-out from the right:

- The ball is in the crook of the stick in the same manner as for pushing out on the left.
- Place your foot directly behind the ball, ensuring it (your right foot) is behind the line. Your foot position relative to the ball is the biggest difference from pushing out on the more traditional right side. The ball is close to the right foot instead of being out in front of the body. The ball and the right foot are very close together. The ball is between the right and left feet but towards the back foot.
- Line your feet up towards the trapper.
- Position the feet shoulder-width apart and get into a squat position. Get low with your weight on the back (right) foot.
- The arms are closer to the body than when you push out on the left, and the left hand ends up very close to the left knee. The action feels a lot more cramped than it does when you're pushing out from the left.
- The stick is not quite parallel with the feet because the left foot is slightly to the left of the right foot. The stick needs to be lined up facing the target so that you can pull it in a straight line towards the trapper.
- From the starting position slowly move the ball forward in the crook of the stick. The initial movement doesn't have to be quick. Keeping the ball in the crook, pull the stick through in a straight line towards the top of the circle. Increase the stick speed as you get the ball moving.

Figure 13.3 (*a*) Push out from the right and get low with your weight on your right back foot which is positioned behind the ball and the stick. (*b*) With the ball in the crook of the stick drag the ball towards the target, leading with your left elbow. (*c*) Follow through in the direction of the target allowing your momentum to take you inside the field of play.

- Transfer your weight from the back foot to the front foot to gain power. It is more difficult to get rotation on this side, but you should try to get as much as possible. (See figure 13.3*a-c*.)

Penalty-Corner Trap

The penalty-corner trapper was often my role in the penalty-corner play. It is a difficult skill to learn, and there are no particular rules for its execution. Sometimes the push-out will be off line, so you need to be mobile and ready to move to the left or the right according to the trajectory of the ball. If the ball is pushed perfectly, you won't need to move your feet at all, except if you choose to step into the ball (down the line as the ball travels towards you). Rest assured, however, that this is another role that largely goes unrewarded when you execute it well, but everyone will notice when you make a mistake!

If you are the penalty-corner trapper, you also need to develop skills other than the basic trap. You need to learn to bunt the ball to another player, dummy as though to bunt, and be ready to 'pick up the crumbs' when and if the penalty corner breaks down. Also, you need to be ready to pounce on rebounds that come to the top of the circle.

When the ball is pushed wide, sometimes you will have the opportunity to trap the ball on your flat stick and have a shot on goal directly. But on most occasions you will be wiser to win another penalty corner and give your team another opportunity to get the set-play execution right.

When you are practicing penalty corners, allocate some session time to playing them out until the ball is out of play. As a team, you need to be proficient at recovering untidy situations that have come about because of occasional skill errors. Be prepared for every eventuality.

Give a target to the player who is pushing the ball into play. As a general rule you will position yourself in the line that you expect and want the ball to travel, allowing one or two steps forward to walk into the trap if that is comfortable for you. You will not need to change your position much if the push-out is accurate.

Many trappers like to stay low to the ground when they are waiting for the ball to arrive, but I always chose to stand up and bend to get low to the ground only once I knew the line on which the ball was travelling. The benefit of staying upright for as long as possible is that you are more mobile than your crouched counterpart, so you can react to a push that is off line more quickly. The benefit other trappers have by starting in the crouched position is that they are prepared earlier for the trap when it is on target. When trapping the ball on a penalty corner, use whatever starting position is most comfortable for you.

As is the case all over the field, concentrate on one skill at a time. First, be very clear early about which variation you and the set-play team are planning to execute, because uncertainty will distract you from the task at hand. Also, if there is a misunderstanding between the trapper and the hitter, it could be a painful experience because in this role your hands are often very close to the hitter's target! Watch the ball as it approaches, and execute the trap and bunt (the skill) before preparing for the next play, just as you would be sure to make a good trap in general play before turning your attention to the next move.

Your decision regarding hand positioning should also come down to personal preference. I liked to start my preparation with my hands apart. My left hand started on the head of the stick, and my right hand was about halfway down the handle, with the hook of the stick pointing towards the ground.

Remember that the palm of your left hand faces the direction from which the ball is travelling and at least your left thumb points towards the hook of the stick. Your fingers can point in this direction also, or you may choose to point them to the ground. Make sure the fingers of your left hand are not wrapped over the top edge of the stick which is the natural thing to do for beginners. (See figure 13.4.) However, many trappers choose to keep their hands together midway down the handle throughout the preparation and skill execution or at least have their hands together (or close together)when the trapping process is underway. (See figure 13.5.)

- When you execute the trap, your stick will be virtually parallel with the ground.
- Angle your stick slightly forward so that the top edge of the stick is forward of the bottom edge as you move with the momentum of the ball. (See figure 13.6.)
- Position your stick so that when you begin to stop the ball (first make contact with the ball), the line on which the ball has travelled is square (at a 90-degree angle) with the stick. (See figure 13.6.)
- If you do these things, (have your stick horizontal and square with the line of the ball with the top edge forward of the bottom edge) you are likely to minimise the extent to which the ball spins as it is controlled and the extent to which it deflects to the side on impact.

In order to have correct body position, line up on the circle so that you trap the ball in a central position that suits the player executing the next skill, such as a hit at the goal. This will give the player taking the shot from the top of the circle the best angle from which to shoot. If you are central, your penalty-corner variations can go to either side of the circle without compromising the eventual shooting angle. You may need to trap the ball slightly to one side of that central position according to the penalty-corner variation that you execute, but be careful not to move too much from the norm, as this will give clues to your opponents regarding your play intentions.

Figure 13.4 Thumb points towards the crook of your stick and your fingers are not wrapped around the top of the stick. Your left palm faces the direction from which the ball is travelling.

Figure 13.5 Hands together for the trap.

Figure 13.6 The stick is parallel with the ground but angled slightly forward and square with the line of the ball at first contact.

Bunting Options

Trapping the ball is only one of the roles for the designated trapper and the subsequent bunting skills are some of the most difficult to get right. The player who traps the ball for penalty corners is usually also the player who bunts or rolls the ball for the next action, such as the hit or the flick. You may bunt the ball over small (5-10 centimetres) or large (3-4 metres) distances, and with varying power to the right, left or straight ahead. You need to also consider the importance of disguising the bunting option that you are going to use.

The Trap and Roll

This is the hard part! Your technique is similar to what we have already discussed in regard to trapping in general play. The idea of catching the ball so as to allow your hands to 'give' as the ball approaches is the same. The only differences are that ultimately your stick will be horizontal for the penalty-corner trap, not vertical as it is in general play, and your hands will be in opposite position (left hand to the left or nearer the head of the stick than the right hand, which is closer to the handle end for this technique). (See figure 13.7a-d.)

Figure 13.7 (*a*) Meet the ball inside the circle. (*b*) Move with the momentum of the ball until the ball is controlled just outside the circle. (*c-d*) Roll the ball into the circle for the hit or next play.

If you 'give' with the ball as it approaches, it will not bounce off your stick as it would if your stick were simply blocking the ball. You will have better control of the ball once it makes contact with your stick if you move with the momentum slightly, and you will be well placed to execute the next skill. Remember these points when catching the ball on the penalty-corner trap:

- Try to meet the ball with your stick before it reaches the top of the circle. This means you may need to step inside the circle for better balance.

- Move your hands and stick backwards with the movement of the ball, until the ball is just outside the circle. The distance that you carry the ball inside the circle may be as much as 30 centimeters (12 inches), depending upon your preference.

- To make the trap and roll as quick as possible, stop the momentum of the ball as close to the outside of the circle as you can after meeting it inside the circle. As you control the ball outside the circle (it does not need to be stopped dead), and if your technique is quick, it may be (depending upon your particular technique) that your stick will not remain square with the line of the ball as you control it because there may not be enough time for your body position to change to accommodate this. Rather, the handle of your stick will likely ultimately point towards the backline and the head away from goal as the ball is stopped (see figure 13.8a). On the other hand you may be able to keep it square which will make the skill easier to execute, but either way, as soon as you have controlled (caught) the ball, roll it back into the circle for the hit or bunt, according to the particular variation of the moment. As you roll it forward for a straight hit variation, your weight may move backwards as you get out of the way of the hitter. Try to increase the speed with which you can catch and roll the ball in a controlled manner. You can practice rolling the ball away from formal training sessions on most surfaces to get the technique right.

77 MEET AND ROLL

Purpose

To become comfortable with the hand position, meeting the ball early and the roll of the ball into the circle.

Procedure

To begin, have someone at close range roll the ball towards you gently. Practice meeting the ball early, controlling it and rolling it forward. Do this repeatedly until you feel comfortable catching the ball and rolling it forward. Increase the distance from which the ball is rolled towards you. Gradually increase the speed of the trap and roll so that it becomes a quick movement.

78 PUSH AND TRAP

Purpose

To put the skills developed in the Meet and Roll drill into practice with a real push-out.

Procedure

Work with the player pushing the ball out, and catch the ball as described in the previous drill. At first, simply make a trap and then add the roll as you feel more comfortable. Repetition is the only way to get better. Increase the speed of the trap and roll as you get better.

The Bunt Left

Bunting, or rolling the ball into the circle for a direct hit or flick, is something that you will need to practice diligently, and again you will need to work with the specific players to whom you are bunting so that you get the angle of the bunt spot on. The players receiving the ball from the bunter (who is also the trapper) can then formulate a routine for their move and fine-tune their timing according to the end position of the ball.

Make sure that the forward bunts into the circle are of a consistent length and angle so that the player executing the next skill can accurately time the hit or flick that follows. This is also the case when bunting the ball to the side for a longer pass. The bunt-pass angles differ according to the specific variations, and each one is important. You can bunt to the left and the right in a number of ways.

The key to bunting left is making sure you control the ball first! Be careful not to be distracted by the second move (the bunt) before you have completed the first step (the trap), in the same way that you make the trap in general play before turning your attention to the next pass or goal shot. Bunt the ball by using the crook of the stick after you control the ball with the trap. (See figure 13.8a-b.) It sounds simple, but usually when a bunting error occurs, it's because you've paid insufficient attention to the detail of the initial trap.

Figure 13.8 (a) Control the ball and (b) use the crook of the stick to bunt the ball.

Sometimes, depending on the variation you have chosen, the later you leave the bunt after you have made the trap, the better. This commits the defensive players to the top of the circle if the hitter executes a convincing dummy at the same time. This gives the player who ultimately receives the bunt more time to execute the shot on goal. Remember that the trap is an important foundation piece for every penalty-corner variation because the ball needs to be controlled before your team is allowed to shoot at goal.

Long Forward Bunt

Another way to bunt to the left is to knock or roll the ball forward into the circle first as though for a 'direct-hit' variation (slightly further forward than for a direct hit). The hitter dummies the hit, and the trapper (confident that the dummy hitter will remember to miss the ball and their stick!) allows the ball to travel forward about a stick length before knocking the ball to the left with the top end (handle end) of the stick. You need to rotate the stick so that it is almost flat on the ground for this part of the skill. It doesn't matter which way you turn the stick—I preferred to have the round side of the stick flat on the ground while others prefer to have the flat side facing down, but the important part to remember is to keep the stick moving close to the ground at all times during the bunt and the follow-through. The bunt usually travels behind the hitter who has followed through as if to execute the hitting motion, towards a player to the left of the battery. (See figure 13.9a-d.)

After the trap and roll forward, rotate the stick so that it is facedown or faceup, depending upon your preference. This allows you to get the stick parallel with and lower to the ground, because the hook of the stick will not raise the stick above the line of the ball. You will get better control and power as a result. Make sure you bunt the ball further into the circle than you would for a normal bunt. This way, you can make contact with the ball

Figure 13.9 (*a*) Knock the ball into the circle as though for a direct hit variation, but slightly longer. (*b*) Rotate your stick so that it is flat on the ground. (*c-d*) At the end of its roll (about one stick length from the trapper), knock the ball with the top of the handle of your stick to the left of the battery keeping the stick flat on the ground.

with the handle of your stick late enough so that the players running out in defence are committed to the ball being hit from the top of the circle. This will make it more difficult for the players running out from the defensive team to make an interception. Your bunt pass will be more effective if you can delay the bunt in this manner. This is a difficult skill, and it takes lots of practice with all the members of the specific set-play combination to get the ball moving on the best angle for the next move.

The Bunt Right

Bunting to the right of the battery is a bit tricky! One way to execute this skill is to pass the ball behind you through your legs. You can dummy over the ball as if to bunt to the left, before knocking the ball behind you and through your legs to your right to be hit by the hitter or the player in the 1R (1st position right of the battery) position. You can also knock the ball to the right across your body using a modified reverse-stick pass.

Hitting off the Trap

Along with the push-out and the trap, this skill provides one of the foundations of the penalty corner. One of the most important things to get right is the timing of the hit with the bunt, so you need to rehearse this with each of the trappers you are likely to play with. You need to develop a routine that is the same every time, no matter which variation is ultimately implemented. This will help to make your skill execution more reliable and will serve to disguise the option that your team elects to use on each occasion.

The hitter needs to practice firing the ball accurately at both corners of the net and also disguise the hit at times so as to make a softer pass for a deflection by a team-mate. This may be in the form of a deliberate 'mis-hit' designed to create a rebound opportunity for the attackers. Not only will this mis-hit give the other offensive players an opportunity to make a deflection, it will also throw off the timing of the goalkeeper, who will expect a full-powered hit from the top of the circle and will move to anticipate this. Matthew Wells is the penalty corner hitter for the Kookaburras. He makes the following points about this important skill:

• Players will differ regarding the position that they want the ball pushed to at the top of the circle. The other thing that will differ slightly from one hitter to another is the length of the bunt from the trapper. Hitters need to rehearse this transition with each combination.

• The stick trappers are the ones who set you up for the strike, so they need to know exactly how long you want the bunt to be.

• I find that the best position for the ball to be delivered at the top of the circle is slightly to the right of the penalty spot so that my hit down the postman side (the right post as I look at it) is straighter and the angle is more open and hasn't been cut down. It also opens up the sideboard on the keeper's stick side (the left as I look at it) and gives me a good-sized target on that side.

Wells describes the key elements to work on with this strike shot:

• Stay relaxed. If you tense up you are likely to mis-hit the ball.
• Know where you want to hit the ball before you hit it.
• Don't try to smash the ball too hard. It's all about the timing and the rhythm that you develop.

One of the hardest skills to develop is the ability to hit the ball over the goalkeeper's stick while at the same time keeping the ball under the 18-inch backboard limit. Hitting down the stick side (the left of the goal as the hitter looks at it) means there is generally no postman in this position because the stick of the goalkeeper is covering that space, so it is all about placement and slight lift or elevation (a couple of inches) rather than power. Like most skills, the hit on the penalty corner requires much practice and repetitive hitting into the corners of the net. Once you build up a rhythm and develop consistent accuracy, you can gradually incorporate more power into the shot and refine the skill.

79   HITTING AT A TARGET

Purpose

To develop a routine and consistency so that you hit with accuracy and power.

Procedure

Place a tyre or a cone in each corner of the net and have a player roll balls into play as the trapper will in a game situation. Before you begin, decide how may balls you will hit into each corner, and aim to do so. Keep your score for 5 or 10 hits, rest, and then begin again. If you have a speed gun, have a coach or a player measure the speed of your hits. Repetition is the only way to improve this important skill. If you are trying to loop the ball, place a small obstacle such as a stick bag in the area where the goalkeeper's stick would be, and try to squeeze the ball over the top, keeping the ball below the backboard.

The Drag Flick

This is an important skill for your team's penalty-corner repertoire. It can be used either off the top of the battery or to the left when the ball is bunted in that direction. Stuart Morgan is a sport scientist at the Victorian Institute of Sport who works with elite hockey players to develop this difficult technique. He makes the following recommendations for the penalty-corner drag flick:

- Grip the stick as though to push the ball.
- Have your left foot approximately level with the ball and your right foot behind the ball.
- Make sure that you are low to the ground (perhaps with your knees bent close to a 90-degree angle) and your stick almost parallel with the ground.
- Place your stick behind the ball and lock your left hand into your right forearm so that your knuckles are touching your forearm and the handle of the stick is pointing behind you.
- Without moving the ball, cross your right leg behind your left leg, then plant your left foot forward of the ball. Only then should you begin to move the ball towards the target using a flicking action.
- Keep your stick on the ball for as long as you can as the ball moves towards the target. This way you are almost 'throwing' the ball from your stick.
- Follow through towards the target.
- The ball should travel to the position that the face of your stick is pointing.

You will generate power for this technique through the momentum of the stepping action in combination with the rotation of the hips and body towards the target. (See figure 13.10*a-e*.)

Figure 13.10 (*a*) Have your left foot approximately level with the ball and your right foot behind the ball. Get low to the ground, lock your left hand into your right forearm and the handle of the stick is pointing behind you. (*b*) Without moving the ball, cross your right leg behind your left leg. (*c-d*) Plant your left foot forward of the ball and then begin to move the ball towards the target using a flicking action. (*e*) Keep your stick on the ball for as long as you can as the ball moves towards the target.

80   DRAG FLICK

Purpose

To practice the flicking technique.

Procedure

Start by flicking a stationary ball from the top of the circle while aiming at the bottom corners of the net. Use targets if you prefer. As you become more comfortable with the technique, aim for the top corners of the net also. Call out which target you aim for each time.

Variation

Have a player bunt the ball as in a flick from the top or to the left of the circle, and pick up the ball to flick it as it moves towards you in the 1L (1st left) position.

Rebounding

Rebounding is an important skill in the penalty-corner repertoire. Some players think that just because they are not part of the initial penalty-corner routine, they are not involved in the penalty-corner execution, and their attention to the penalty corner suffers as a result. This is a risky misconception! Very rarely does the direct shot on goal or the first shot on goal from a penalty-corner variation actually get past a 'well-oiled' penalty-corner defence.

KEY NOTE
Often the players who are alert and ready for the ball to rebound to them from the initial shot score the goals.

The principles of rebounding in general play apply (see chapter 7):

- Keep your weight moving forward.
- Keep your weight on the balls (toes) of your feet.
- Keep your stick and body position low to the ground (low centre of gravity).
- Expect and 'will' the ball to come to you.

In this set-play situation you have better information about where the ball is likely to fall than you do in general play, because you know which variation will occur. This is why it is critical that all players on the attacking circle during a penalty corner gather together before the corner and share the information about which variation has been selected. If you know exactly where on the circle the shot on goal will be coming from, you can anticipate the likely rebound area with greater confidence than your opponents can because you have prior knowledge of the likely angles.

Some penalty-corner variations may be planned so that the ball rebounds to a particular area in the circle. A good rebounding player can be in a position on the circle top so that he can move to that particular area and knock the ball into the net. This is a set play, as is a direct hit from the top of the circle.

81 — REBOUNDING ON PENALTY CORNERS

Purpose

To become comfortable with the likely rebounding angles and to practice timing your run from the top of the circle to be in position to pounce on the ball.

Procedure

Start your run from the position on the circle that you will come from in a match situation, and time your run according to the position you want to get to. A player hits the ball at a goalkeeper or a rebound board (count one for the push-out, two for the trap and three for the hit to get the timing right), and the rebounder gets to rebounding position as quickly as possible beginning her run once the number 1 is called. To make your run more realistic, you can put obstacles in the place that you think defenders will be. Practice this skill with the player who will make the original shot in the game so that you can get the timing right according to his technique and the speed of the shot. When possible, practice with a real goalkeeper to get the rebounding angles right. The best practice is a full penalty-corner attack against a full defence.

Deflecting

KEY NOTE
A player ready to make a deflection can widen the goal for the attacking team.

This skill is important in penalty-corner situations. A deft touch from a hit or a push at goal or a pass into the attacking circle can be enough to beat even the best penalty-corner defence. Players who can deflect the ball well become critical to completing the penalty-corner set-up. These players usually make a beeline for a position in front of the goalposts or even across the face of goal, and they can sometimes serve to distract the defenders enough so that the initial shot on goal is effective. Often these sneaky players change the line of the ball travelling towards the goal or wide of it, just late enough to prevent the goalkeeper from reacting in time.

Deflecting is a difficult skill because the pass needs to be fast, flat and accurate, but sometimes this does not happen. If one of these variables is off the mark, you will have very little time to react and change position, or a defender may get to the ball first.

The circle is a crowded area during a penalty-corner play, and often it is difficult for the player on the receiving end of the pass to see the ball perfectly. As a deflector placed deep in the attacking circle, you may be unsighted when up to 15 players at any given time (attacking and defensive players) set up in a congested area. Therefore, you need to be particularly alert.

KEY NOTE
Sacrifice distance for balance when positioning to make a deflection on a penalty corner.

Get as close as you can to the perfect position as soon as you can, but remember that you will be better served if you are balanced as the ball approaches than if you are closer to the goal and unbalanced.

By *balanced*, I mean that you are no longer moving quickly, you have a wide base because your feet are spread comfortably, you have a low centre of gravity and you can focus your attention on getting the stick to the ball. A wide, low base also gives you strength over the ball and makes you less vulnerable to the push of a defender. Hold your ground! Give the player passing the ball a clear target and you can adjust your position according to the set-up of the penalty-corner defence.

Practice getting to position and receiving the ball from the player who is likely to make the pass in the game situation, because as is the case for all set-play variations, success will come when all players have a good understanding of the movements and positional preferences of all the players involved.

82   DEFLECTING ON PENALTY CORNERS

Purpose

To get your timing right for the approach to the deflection.

Procedure

As soon as the ball is pushed into the circle (if you don't have the 'pusher-outer' and a trapper, have someone call 'Push out and trap'), get to your deflecting position as quickly as possible according to those calls. Then set up a target for the player passing the ball. Keep your back to the sideline and make the deflection. Do this from both sides of the circle. To begin, just position yourself in the circle without running in, and have balls hit at you to practice getting a touch on the ball.

All contributors within the corner battery have their idiosyncrasies in the ways they like to receive the ball and position their bodies as they do so. As a result, each passer and deflector has slightly different timing issues and techniques that will make a difference in the exact execution of the variation.

Deflections can be made on both sides of the goal. If you are deflecting from the right of the goal, allow the ball to hit your stick on your flat side, presuming the hit is accurate and in front of you. If you are running in from the left of the attacking circle, you have two options:

1. Make the deflection on your flat stick. I think this option is preferable for a basic deflection on the left post, because you can connect with the ball in front of your body and watch the ball all the way as it approaches. It is the safest and simplest technique for executing the deflection with precision, but it requires perfect position and perfect delivery of the ball. (See figure 13.11.)

2. Make the deflection on your reverse side. If you make a deflection with your reverse stick on the left post, you can lose sight of it at the last moment as it travels across your body from the top of the circle. It is more difficult to make good or 'thick' contact with the ball in this instance. However, you will need to use this technique if you are late getting into position, you need to

Figure 13.11   Flat stick-deflection.

reach or dive for the ball, or if the hit is more central (closer to the centre of the goal) than you expected. Be aware that you will make contact with the ball later than you would for the first alternative, which reduces your choice of angles for the deflection. (See figure 13.12.)

Figure 13.12   Reverse-stick deflection.

On other occasions the ball will be deliberately hit towards the centre of the goal, and in this instance you need to deflect the ball from both sides of the goal with your stick outstretched. In this situation it is likely that you will look to deflect the ball over the goalkeeper, who has gone to ground. This can occur from both sides, but the technique will differ so that on the right side you deflect the ball on your flat stick and on the left side you have the option of the forestick and reverse-stick techniques. In both instances you will place your stick in the line of the ball and angle it slightly to achieve the desired elevation—usually to deflect over a goalkeeper who is lying down.

Using Signals

It sometimes makes sense to nominate the people who play one particular role in an attacking penalty corner as the designated players to read the signals from the bench. This will eliminate confusion and conjecture about the options, and it frees up the other players to concentrate on their upcoming roles in the corner.

For example, perhaps only the trapper looks for the signal, and the other players focus on preparing for the execution of each skill. It doesn't matter which player takes this role. Similarly, it doesn't matter which personnel are on the field at the time because there will always be one player or another who is assuming the nominated role.

The coach or another nominated player might use his hands to touch his head, feet, the chair next to him, or some other body part or object to give signals. You will need to change the signals, the objects, or the person giving the signal regularly so that your opponents don't start to predict your signals.

DEFENDING PENALTY CORNERS

KEY NOTE
Your best penalty-corner defence is to avoid giving them away at all!

The defending team uses five players for the penalty-corner defence. All players must remain behind the goal line until the attacking team pushes the ball into play, but the defending team can set up in any position on the back line. This will vary according to the playing personnel on both teams and the likely attacking options that will be used. Be careful not to break (the defensive runners take off before the ball is pushed into the field of play) as the umpires may eventually penalise your team with a penalty stroke although you are likely to be warned before this happens.

If you tackle outside the defensive 25-yard area when possible, you will limit the number of corners you give away. An untidy or deliberate foul within this defensive area will result in the umpire's awarding a penalty corner, whereas a tackle outside the 25 will probably not be punished so harshly.

Penalty Corner Defensive Options

The chosen method of penalty-corner defence will depend largely on the strengths and weaknesses of the attacking team in combination with the strengths and weaknesses of your defensive unit. You can vary the details of these methods of penalty-corner defence. Generally, your team has two options in the defensive penalty-corner set-up:

1. **1:3**—One fast runner and three field players holding back. This variation involves the first runner going straight to the battery at the top of the circle to try to block the direct shot. The second runner trails behind the first to an area level with the penalty spot mark but outside the line of the left post. The third player from the right comes out to a position that is goal side of the penalty spot, again outside the line of the post. The fourth defender lines up level with the goalkeeper's feet on the left post and is responsible for making a save on the line or clearing the goalkeeper's pads. The second and third players are responsible for stopping opposition players getting in close to the goalkeeper for deflection and rebound opportunities.

The goalkeeper also has the option of running to the top of the circle. This is becoming an increasingly popular option with the improved ability of players (particularly in the men's game) to drag-flick the ball from the trap. Alternatively, the goalkeeper can stay in the net and lie down or stand up to defend a raised shot on goal.

This type of defence is mostly used when the opposition has one good striker at the top of the circle, if it uses several variations, or if it has players who are good at deflecting on penalty corners. The 1:3 style of defence leaves the position to the left of the battery (1L) quite vulnerable. (See figure 13.13.)

2. **2:2**—Two fast runners. The first two runners go directly to the top of the circle—usually one to the battery and the other to the 1L position. The other two defenders stay back closer to the goal. The player on the left post is level with the goalkeeper, and the player on the right post is slightly forward of the goalkeeper. Both these deep players need to be aware of opposition players lurking for deflections, and they are also responsible for clearing the goalkeeper's pads. The 2:2 defence is used when the opposition team has two good striking options at the top of the circle (strong batteries). The vulnerable area is to the right of the circle in the deflecting and rebounding positions. (See figure 13.14.)

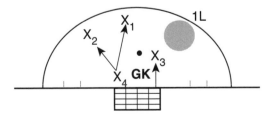

Figure 13.13 1:3 defence.

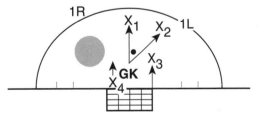

Figure 13.14 2:2 defence.

83   PENALTY-CORNER DEFENCE REHEARSAL

Purpose

To rehearse and evaluate the exact positioning of the players in the penalty-corner defense.

Procedure

Set up the defence without an attacking team. The coach calls the push-out, and the players assume their positions according to the particular variation that is called (1:3 or 2:2, for example). Everyone is stationary by the time the ball would reach the top of the circle and the relative positioning of the players is assessed. Do this for the two basic defensive penalty-corner variations we have discussed and any others that you come up with. You can vary the starting position of the players as you wish.

Goalkeeper's Role

Decide early which defensive structure your team will assume in order to defend the penalty corner. This means that as a goalkeeper you will either stand up to make the initial save, lie down to block the first shot on goal, or run to the top of the circle to block a likely flick from the top of the circle. Justine Sowry recommends that unless you are playing at the highest level, it's best to stand for the initial shot because at most levels of the game there will be very few players who can hit past you. In this situation you are more mobile for the next save. If you lie down to make the initial save, do so from one knee (one knee on the ground) or from a standing position, but only once the hitter is committed to the shot. Once you are committed to going to ground, it will be difficult to react successfully to a high ball. So you should get back to an upright position as quickly as possible once the ball is cleared from the pads. The goalkeeper should try to read the variation early and call it to the other players if there is time. The rebound should be directed into a safe position for the defensive team (preferably out of the circle).

Postie Role

Hockeyroo Katie Allen is an expert in defensive penalty-corner trapping (on the post), just as she is very good at trapping in general play. She says that the principles for trapping in the field apply for the penalty-corner trap, but she outlines the following additional points for the important penalty-corner 'postie' role:

- Be ready and want the ball to come to you. Uncertainty or hesitation will hinder your ability to make a clean trap, and it may result in a goal to the opposition. One coach I had likened post trapping to fielding in the 'slips' position in the game of cricket. As is the case for goal shooting, you can go an entire day and may only have one chance, so you need to expect that every ball will come to you so that you are ready for when it does come your way.

- It may help to have a routine you learn to follow every time. That may mean counting the number of steps off the goal line that you take each time you assume your position, and then getting balanced in the same place each time. This allows you to have a single focus on the ball because the process becomes instinctive and limits the possible distractions.

'Most of our hockey is played on synthetic surfaces these days, so we often take it for granted that the ball will be delivered to us flat along the ground. We assume that the trap will be made, and we consequently begin planning our next move (a pass, dribble or elimination skill) before we actually have control of the ball. Neglecting to pay enough attention to the trap is a common cause of the ever-frustrating and genuinely costly "mis-trap." '
—Katie Allen

Penalty corners are important elements of the game; but so many variables can go wrong, which can be very frustrating. You need to practice each attacking skill as individuals, then combine them to develop successful attacking variations. The push-out and the trap are particularly critical because, until these are completed successfully, the remainder of the variation cannot come into play. On occasion you will score from a 'mucked-up' corner, but you need to develop a coordinated corner battery to maximise your chances. Similarly, the defence of corners is critical and requires much coordination and practice as a unit.

It is unlikely that each player would be expected to be an expert in more than one or two positions on each of the attacking and defensive corners, but a general awareness of all the skills is still useful and will make you a more flexible and useful player. So many different skills are involved, so there is something for everyone. Remember, the more skills you can offer the team, the more valuable you will be as a player.

CHAPTER 14

PEAK PLAYER FITNESS

The game of hockey brings into play all elements of physical fitness, injury maintenance and nutrition. Successful hockey players have a good level of aerobic fitness to enable them to last the duration of the game. They warm up before every training session or game and cool down afterwards, and they eat well to keep themselves at peak fitness.

PEAK PHYSICAL FITNESS

You may wonder how fit you need to be to play hockey. That depends entirely on the level of hockey that you aspire to play. Naturally, the higher the level of competition, the faster the speed of the game, and the fitter you must be.

To be a good field hockey player, you must be able to do the following:

- Keep up with the pace of the game when on the field.
- Remain on the field, free of injury and fatigue.
- Be available for selection and present a strong case for selection so that you can get onto the field and show your skills.

Of course, few athletes are strong in all areas of physical fitness. For example, rarely is an athlete fast over short distances (10 to 15 metres) as well as able to endure long distances, but you can improve your base level of all these components by making a committed effort over time. Denise Jennings, physical preparation coordinator at the Victorian Institute of Sport and former elite hockey player, provides insight into the following discussion on speed, aerobic and anaerobic ability, and agility. Her significant contribution to this chapter will help you develop a training program for overall fitness, with special consideration of your specific position.

Speed

It's unlikely that many players in your team are lightning quick over all distances. Some might be very explosive over a distance of 10 metres, whereas others have the ability to accelerate over a longer distance and maintain that speed for a longer period. Both abilities are valuable assets, but the value of each depends on the position you play.

Short, sharp speed is necessary in the midfield when players are looking to break lines in confined space, but the outright attackers (strikers) and defenders need to be quickest over both short and longer distances. Speed is critical for strikers who look to break from their immediate opponents and necessary also for defenders who need to catch a breakaway forward or get back in cover defence.

The key areas for speed development are as follows:

1. Distance covered
2. Intensity of effort (percentage of maximum effort)
3. Rest between each effort (work-to-rest ratio)

KEY NOTE
You need to be completely rested between efforts to maintain the intensity at 100 percent and improve your explosive speed off the mark.

To maximise the specificity of training for hockey, at practice you should replicate the distances you cover in the game. The majority of high-intensity efforts or sprints are performed over distances of 5 to 15 metres. Longer efforts do occur, but they are the exception rather than the rule. When you're developing speed, the first two to three steps are critical. This sharp acceleration could be the difference between getting a stick to the ball and being beaten to the ball by your opponent. The intensity of each effort is also critical. To develop speed you must give efforts of 100 percent. Anything less will compromise the extent to which you improve. As a result, the rest period for this training is longer than that used to develop repeated sprint efforts.

Figure 14.1 shows a sample session for developing speed.

Figure 14.1 Sample Speed Session

Warm-up, including sprint drills and dynamic stretching

4 × 20 m sprints at 100% effort with 1-2 min breaks between each sprint

3 × 15 m falling start sprints with 1-2 min breaks between sprints

6 × 10 m sprints with different start positions with 1 min break between efforts

Cool-down jog plus stretches

Aerobic Fitness

Strong aerobic fitness is critical, particularly for players in the midfield. But all field players need a strong aerobic base from which to develop other physiological abilities. A strong aerobic ability allows you to run all day and gives you the best opportunity to recover from sprint efforts.

Fatigue can affect the quality of your skill execution, but the frequency with which this occurs can be limited with a good aerobic base. Aerobic fitness also maximises your ability to recover between each sprint effort. This helps you to execute your skills with precision in the later stages of the game.

The following methods of training are commonly used for developing the aerobic base:

1. Continuous training at a constant elevated heart rate within a range of 140 to 160 beats per minute. You can determine the training zone by using the formula of 220 minus your age (your maximum heart rate) multiplied by .60 to .80. More experienced and elite athletes will be able to have a better 'feel' for their particular training zone from their own experience and training years.
2. Fartlek training.
3. Interval-based sessions.

Continuous Training

Continuous, or steady-state, training involves performing a steady, constant, low-intensity activity for longer than 10 minutes. Usually, for the development of an aerobic base for a team sport, durations of 20 to 60 minutes are optimal at the level of intensity described earlier. Because hockey is a running-based sport, running is the preferred method of training. But cycling and swimming can also improve this energy system. Keep in mind that the continuous nature of this style of training does not replicate the game of hockey, which involves running at various speeds and in different directions. So, you need to do aerobic training in combination with other forms of training.

Note that aerobic training may impede your speed development. As a result, this training is best performed in the off-season when speed development is not emphasised so much in training.

Fartlek Training

This physical training is a continuous session (usually running), but it includes a variety of intensity efforts that replicate those efforts in the game of hockey. Figure 14.2 shows a sample of fartlek training.

Figure 14.2   Sample Fartlek Training

5 min: jogging warm-up and stretching
5 min: continuous running
5 min: jog 50 sec; sprint 10 sec (85% effort); repeat for 5 min
5 min: jog
5 min: jog 50 m, stride (75% effort) 50 m; jog 50 m; stride 50 m; repeat for 5 min
5 min: jog
5 min: sprint 20 m, jog backwards 10 m, stride 50 m, jog 100 m, repeat for 5 min
Cool-down: slow jogging and stretching

Many activities can be included in a fartlek session: agility circuits, various efforts of intensity, backwards and forwards running and even skill training. Fartlek training is much more specific to hockey than a long, continuous running session because it more closely replicates the physical requirements of the game. Implementation of these sessions is limited only by your imagination, so you can be creative with fartlek and interval training.

Interval Training

Interval training involves using higher-intensity sprint efforts interspersed with rest periods. This type of training develops the following:

- The *aerobic base* is necessary for playing team sports such as hockey.
- The *anaerobic energy system* increases your ability to perform repeated sprint efforts with minimal rest.

Keep in mind the following two concepts when developing an interval session:

1. Work done. This is measured either by distance or time taken to implement the effort or the intensity of each effort.
2. Rest taken. This is the amount of rest prescribed between each effort.

The combination of these two areas determines the work-to-rest ratio, which determines how difficult a session will be. The lower the ratio, the harder the session, whereas a higher ratio prescribes more rest per effort, so it is easier. The particular stage of physical preparation of the team or individual will determine the best ratio in each instance.

The length of an interval effort also varies according to the time of year or stage and emphasis of the training phase. Earlier in preseason, longer intervals of 200 to 300 metres (220 to 330 yards) would be used with rest periods of up to 3 minutes. Sessions closer to the start of the season will require the distances of each interval to shorten to 5 to 20 metres (about 5.5 to 22 yards) of high-intensity efforts, with shorter breaks of only 10 to 20 seconds interspersed. You can manipulate interval training to simulate the physical characteristics of a hockey game. Therefore, interval training is the best type of physical training to use to train for match conditions.

See figures 14.3 and 14.4 for examples of an interval training session.

Figure 14.3   Interval Training Session 1

Warm-up and stretching (see warm-up protocols)
4 × 150 m (75-85% effort) with 3:1 recovery-to-effort ratio
(if effort takes 25 sec, rest = 75 sec)
2 min rest between each set
4 × 120 m (85% effort) with 3:1 recovery-to-effort ratio
2 min rest
3 × 100 m (90% effort) with 4:1 recovery-to-effort ratio
Cool-down: jogging and stretching

Figure 14.4   Interval Training Session 2

Warm-up and stretching
60 m, 40 m, 20 m, 40 m, 60 m (100% effort) with walk-back recovery
2 min rest
10 m, 15 m, 20 m, 15 m, 10 m (100% effort) with walk-back recovery
2 min rest
4 × 15 m sprints (100% effort) with 4:1 recovery-to-effort ratio
Cool-down: 5 min slow jogging and stretching

Anaerobic Ability

Anaerobic, or 'without oxygen,' requires large bursts of energy over shorter periods. During anaerobic exercise, stored fuels such as glycogen provide energy at a fast rate without the need for oxygen. All players need to perform intense physical efforts with a lot of stopping and starting, thus using their anaerobic abilities. Goalkeepers in particular may only have a couple of passages where they are directly involved in a match, and in these instances they may be required to repeat efforts and then stop.

Good anaerobic fitness enables you to repeat sprints throughout the game. Players involved in any position need sound anaerobic fitness. It's especially vital for players who wish to play in the midfield because they need to cover so much territory over the course of the match. Midfielders might run up to 12 kilometres (7.5 miles) per game which is made up of short sprints and efforts of between 3 and 30 metres, with periods of jogging and even walking, which the body uses as valuable recovery from the more intensive efforts. The ability to sprint into attack or chase into defence for the whole game with speed and without fatigue is important for midfielders playing at any level. Develop this system using the interval method (explained previously), which involves short, high-intensity efforts that simulate what happens in the game. Anaerobic training will allow for the development of speed as well as endurance in a sport-specific manner.

Agility

The ability to change direction quickly over a short distance is important for forwards as they look to eliminate their immediate opponents. Of course, agility is also important for the defenders who need to react to this movement. Midfielders, as well as goalkeepers, need to move with some dynamism in tight situations.

Eun-Jin Kim from Korea dives at the ball and away from Great Britain's Pauline Stott.

Making the Most of Every Practice Session

Fitness activities within drills make for good use of your time and energy while closely replicating the physically demanding nature of the game. If you have chosen to take hockey seriously, you have no doubt done so because you enjoy the many challenges of the game, so you don't want your training to feel more like that of a track athlete! Therefore, you will want to minimise the amount of extra time outside of training sessions that you spend taking care of important elements of fitness.

To maximise your efficiency and enjoyment of the game, you can often combine your skill and fitness sessions. This will benefit your game simultaneously because you will become more adept at skill execution when you are in a fatigued state. The development of fitness is hard work, but it is amazing how much easier it is to do the hard physical training in a team environment. In this way your mind is distracted by the skills of the game, which are the components of the game that you really enjoy. For example, if you're on the training track for 60 minutes, make sure you are active for much of that time. If your training session is well planned, you can do a low-intensity activity such as a slow jog around the field as you collect balls between drills and rehydrate as the coach sets up the next task. If you are in a training phase that concentrates on aerobic development, this continuous training style is particularly relevant.

Similarly, when you are looking to develop speed and acceleration off the mark, be sure to take these elements into consideration when you are chasing the ball or opponents at training. Make a 100 percent effort while you are at training, and you won't need to do so much physical training at other times.

INJURY PREVENTION AND MAINTENANCE

Warm-ups, stretching and recovery are important components of your preparation and post session routine, which will help to prevent injury and ensure that you recover quickly for the next game or training session. But sometimes injuries are unavoidable, and they present in many ways. Injuries vary from small and annoying niggles to chronic, debilitating injuries. Sometimes it is difficult for athletes to admit to themselves and the coach that there is a problem because they are competitive and they want to play the game that they enjoy so much.

You need to be honest with yourself and recognise injury concerns early on to minimise the ultimate effect of the injury. This will give you the best opportunity to achieve playing longevity.

In my time with the Hockeyroos, Kate Starre was suffering from a chronic back injury. She was extremely diligent when it came to her rehabilitation. As a result, in a 200-plus game career, she never missed a major tournament because of injury. Not many players in the group could make this claim. Here are Kate's tips for injury management:

1. Maintain general fitness while you are injured so that your comeback is not so difficult. There is usually something that you can do to maintain your fitness.

2. Accept that rehabilitation can be boring, but you *must* do it. To minimise the boredom factor, do it in front of the TV or any place where you can be entertained.

3. Don't isolate yourself from your team-mates because you are injured. Stay involved and be positive.

Warm-Ups

The warm-up prepares the body physically and psychologically for the training or game environment. It includes cardiorespiratory, muscular and neural preparation specific to the needs of the training session or the match. Neural training refers to the nervous system and the ability of the nerves to activate the muscles and initiate a muscular effort such as firing the muscles to perform an activity which is especially important for activities such as hockey that require sprinting or explosive efforts.

The warm-up serves the following purposes:

1. Improves performance
2. Reduces the risk of injury
3. Activates specific motor units
4. Provides an opportunity for skill rehearsal
5. Promotes psychological preparation

The warm-up process has evolved to become more dynamic and more specific to the requirements of the game or training session. No longer is static stretching a significant component of the warm-up; rather, it is replaced with a series of dynamic exercises designed to mimic specific movements associated with the game of hockey.

Players begin with low-intensity activities (for example, jogging and simple movements associated with the game) and progressively build the intensity. These low-intensity exercises may include the following:

- Heel flicks
- High knees
- Grapevine
- Backwards running

Next the focus should be on aerobic activity that enhances the sport-specific skills for technique and competition, such as playing a small game that encourages similar movements to those required during the game.

- Training-specific exercises. This phase of the warm-up incorporates exercises that are specific to the game or training. The ranges of motion that players will perform within the upcoming session or game need to be replicated in a dynamic manner rather than with a static stretch. Exercises might include jogging combined with ground touches every couple of metres, drills that emphasize change of direction, short accelerations across the field and sprint relays between the team members.

- Competition-specific exercises. These exercises replicate the skill component of the game, such as set plays and skill-based exercises that are performed at game intensity. Warm-up drills include pushing, hitting, trapping, tackling, 1v1 drills, team-based passing drills and short corner practise. Playing 3-on-3 or 4-on-4 games is also an effective way to prepare for the game. Soccer, touch football or other games where players are jogging, performing cutting movements, running backwards and higher-intensity efforts are excellent warm-up games for hockey players. These also provide variety and an element of fun and variation to the warm-up process.

The activities and duration involved in the warm-up vary according to the ages, interests and condition of your players. Finally, remember to vary the warm-ups so that you don't get bored with the routine.

Position-Specific Fitness

As in most team sports, each 'line' or group of players—strikers, midfielders, defenders, and goalkeepers—has slightly different fitness requirements. Players in each position must train to perform the specific physical requirements of their positions. For example, it is of little value to the team to have midfielders who can run all day in a steady state but can't sprint forward into attack, or deep defenders who can't keep up with their opposition forwards.

- Strikers. Strikers need to be able to run at speed so that they can burst into attack. They also need to be able to do this repeatedly throughout the game, not only at the beginning of each half. An underlying level of aerobic fitness is required, but the emphasis of the strikers' fitness program lies in speed development and the ability to repeat sprints through anaerobic training. It is of little use for strikers to continue with long, slow, continuous running during the season, as this type of activity is foreign to them during the game and will limit the extent to which they improve their speed.

- Midfielders. These players are sometimes called the workhorses who make up the engine room of the team. They're the link between the strikers and defenders and are often the top possession-getters in a match. The majority of these players' efforts involve jogging (strides of 65 to 75 percent of maximum effort) as well as shorter bursts of speed to support their strikers in attack, break lines in the midfield and chase their opposition players into defence. Midfielders need higher levels of aerobic fitness than any other players on the ground, but they should not neglect their anaerobic development. Specificity is still the key. Long, slow, steady-state running only makes midfielders better at long, slow, steady-state running. If they're expected to perform fast, explosive sprints and accelerate into attack, then their training must reflect these types of efforts.

- Defenders. At the back of the field the deep defenders require the ability to keep up with the explosive strikers, and they need sharp footwork and agility to tackle and backtrack when in one-on-one tackling situations. Again, an underlying aerobic component is part of the defenders' make-up, but just as important is their ability to match the physical attributes of the strikers, which is sprint-and-recovery based. Defenders' training programs must address footwork and agility because the ability to perform these movements with quality while fatigued can turn a game.

- Goalkeepers. The physical requirements of the goalkeeper are different to those of any of their team-mates, so goalkeepers should train accordingly. Explosive speed and agility, both laterally and vertically, are characteristics necessary for goalkeepers to perform at the highest level. Aerobic fitness is not a big part of a goalkeeper's program; however, a moderate level will help them to sustain efforts that enable them to train at a higher level. Speed development is the key, and goalkeepers should train these skills in and out of goalkeeping equipment.

The focus of the warm-up depends on the desired outcome of the warm-up. The duration of a training warm-up as opposed to a match warm-up will also be shorter, and in some instances the warm-up may not be performed on the field of play because the field may not be available.

Other factors affecting your warm-up might include the climate and athletic conditioning of the players.

• Climate. The climate in which the training session or tournament is conducted has a bearing on the duration of the warm-up. In warmer climates or in summer months the warm-up time can be reduced, as the warm environment naturally warms the body's muscles and increases circulation. In warm weather, you'll need to schedule more drink breaks throughout the warm-up, and you may need to increase the amount of rest during drills.

• Athletes' conditioning. Level of overall fitness in athletes also has an effect on the duration and quality of the warm-up. The fitter the athletes, the better they will be able to tolerate the overall warm-up without becoming fatigued. It may be necessary to modify warm-up procedures for players who are not as fit as their team-mates.

As a tournament or competition progresses, players may become fatigued, and they may need to modify the duration of the warm-up; however, it's still important to maintain the intensity.

Flexibility

A certain level of flexibility, which relies on muscle length and range of motion (ROM) in the joints, is necessary for hockey players. This sport can predispose athletes to tightness and muscle imbalances in certain parts of the body, which may lead to altered and less efficient movement patterns within the body and eventually to overuse injuries such as low back pain, knee pain, shin splints and stress fractures. Addressing specific flexibility needs for each player and creating good habits will maximise the enjoyment and longevity in players' careers. Following are some guidelines for stretching:

• Perform each stretch *at least* twice on each side.
• Hold each stretch for *at least* 60 seconds.
• Warm up by jogging for approximately five minutes before stretching.
• You can also use stretches as a cool-down after a game or training.

Recovery

Successful athletes train hard to achieve their goals. To withstand the intensities of training and to have the opportunity to accumulate game time, you must follow guidelines for regeneration and recovery.

Recovery management allows your body time to adapt to the benefits of training. If there is insufficient time for recovery before the next training session, your body will not recover its capacity before the next session. If this occurs, your ability to perform a high-quality training session will be compromised. If you are continually overloaded without sufficient rest or the implementation of specific recovery strategies, injury and burnout may occur.

The following are the methods used in the recovery process:

• Massage
• Hydrotherapy

KEY NOTE
Incorporating longer rest intervals in the warm-up while maintaining the intensity of each effort is one way to combat a build-up of fatigue.

KEY NOTE
Never underestimate the psychological benefit of the warm-up process. Remember that a warm-up is about preparing both physically and mentally for the tasks ahead.

- Hot and cold contrast techniques
- Nutrition and hydration
- Rest
- Mental relaxation techniques
- Planning of sessions and recovery within sessions

First 5 minutes after exercise: Recover your energy.
- Drink and eat. (See the section on nutrition.)
- Stretch while warm. Use static or partner stretching.
- Walk or move lightly. Jog or cycle 5 to 10 minutes.
- Check weight for fluid loss.

First 5 to 10 minutes after exercise: Recover physically.
In the shower:
- Stretch and self-massage.
- Alternate between hot and cold water (2 to 3 minutes hot, 30 seconds cold).

First hour after exercise: Continue to recover.
- Drink plenty of fluid.
- Have something else to eat.
- Relax and unwind.

In the evening:
- Take a hot shower or spa.
- Stretch or self-massage.
- Continue to hydrate.

As a coach, you'll need to develop a schedule of training sessions, particularly for junior players who may be competing in several sports, teams and squads. If players arrive at training in a fatigued state because of the volume of training sessions in each week, it may be necessary to prioritise sessions and introduce some flexibility or compromise in training commitments. It will help to develop a plan outlining all sessions during a typical week. This might include other sports, school commitments and club, team and representative commitments. Overloading junior athletes may eventually lead to overuse injuries and burnout, which will affect their development as hockey players.

Intrasession recovery is also an important component of the recovery process. You can manipulate rest periods within sessions to monitor and determine the intensity of each drill. Using drink breaks is an excellent way to monitor the intensity of sessions and also provide hydration opportunities for the players. If you have them, heart rate monitors are useful here too.

NUTRITION

Preparing for a game or training session and providing appropriate nutrition for the replenishment of fluid and fuel stores used in training require planning by athletes and coaches. The following are examples of suitable meals and snacks for athletes at various times in a training or game day.

Pregame

The following food choices are suitable to eat three to four hours before exercise. Choose one:

- Crumpets with jam or honey and flavoured milk
- Baked potato with cottage cheese filling and a glass of milk
- Baked beans on toast
- Breakfast cereal with milk
- Bread roll with cheese or meat filling and a banana
- Fruit salad with fruit-flavoured yoghurt
- Pasta or rice with a low-fat sauce (such as tomato, vegetables, lean meat)

The following snacks are suitable to eat one to two hours before exercise:

- Fruit cereal bars
- Milkshake or fruit smoothie
- Sports bars (check labels for carbohydrate, fat and protein content)
- Breakfast cereal with milk
- Fruit-flavoured yoghurt

Planning and effort are required in order to attain peak playing fitness.

Postgame

Within 30 minutes of the end of the session, the replenishment of carbohydrate stores should be the focus. Therefore, players, coaches and parents must plan ahead to arrange post-training meals. This can be as simple as packing a banana or sports drink to enhance the overall recovery process. The following are some more meal options.

Carbohydrate-rich recovery snacks (50-gram portions of carbohydrate)
- 700 to 800 millilitres (24 to 28 ounces) of sports drink
- 500 millilitres (18 ounces) of fruit juice or soft drink
- 2 slices of toast or bread with jam or honey or banana topping
- 2 cereal bars
- 1 cup thick vegetable soup and large bread roll
- 1 large or 2 small (115 grams) American muffins, fruit buns or scones
- 300 grams creamed rice
- 1 large (300 grams) baked potato with salsa filling

- 2 pancakes (100 grams) with 30 grams of syrup
- 250 to 300 millilitres (9 to 11 ounces) of milkshake or fruit smoothie

By drinking fluid regularly during exercise, you can prevent declines in skill level and concentration and excessive elevations in heart rate and body temperature; therefore, you can improve performance. Rehydrating does not come naturally to all players, so coaches can facilitate this important component by doing the following:

- Recognise the importance of fluid replacement during exercise.
- Educate players regarding hydration.
- Help players prepare a fluid-replacement plan for training and competition.
- Incorporate opportunities for rehydration during training.
- Provide cool, flavoured, palatable drinks that are readily accessible during training and competition.
- Establish team rules designed to encourage fluid intake (for example, all athletes must bring suitable fluids or a drink bottle to training).
- Assess fluid balance during training sessions to help athletes determine individual fluid losses. Athletes can weigh themselves pre- and post-sessions to evaluate their fluid loss. This is a cheap and practical way to do so in hot environments.

Playing fitness (general health, strength, speed and aerobic ability) is a major contributor to the development of a high-quality player. If you consider that the skills presented in earlier chapters are necessary for playing the game, you can see that your physical conditioning allows you to get on, and stay on, the field to use those skills.

Physical conditioning helps you avoid injury and allows you more time on the field before fatigue sets in. The types of fitness required differ according to the position that you play. Regardless, a benefit of being physically fit applies to all field players: Even if your ball-handling skills are below par on a given day, you can still run and chase hard. Good physical conditioning and smart nutrition give you an edge, even when you feel as though your skills have deserted you. Physical fitness can be hard work, but if you plan your sessions and train in a group you can make it more enjoyable and you will certainly be rewarded for your effort by your improved performances on the field.

◻ **INDEX** ◻

Note: The italicized *f* following page numbers refers to figures.

◻ **ABOUT THE AUTHOR** ◻

Claire Mitchell-Taverner, OAM, broke into the Australian national team in 1993 and was a consistent member of the Telstra Hockeyroos women's field hockey team through a period in which they were described as Australia's most successful sports team ever.

With 180 international matches and 47 goals to her credit, Mitchell-Taverner has been rated one of the world's best female goal-scoring midfielders over the past decade. She retired from international competition in 2001.

Mitchell-Taverner has been a member of gold medal-winning teams at all international-level hockey tournaments. From 1992 to 2000, the Hockeyroos won gold medals in every international competition they entered, including the Olympic Games (2000), World Cup (1998), Commonwealth Games (1998), and Champions Trophy (1995-1999). They took the bronze in the 2000 Champions Trophy tournament.

Mitchell-Taverner enjoys sharing her love for the game and her knowledge of it by coaching and speaking at corporate functions, sports clubs, and schools. She has been on several television and radio shows and serves as the expert hockey commentator on major events for ABC Radio in Australia. She is also a regular contributor and columnist for the *Sunday Age*.

Claire has two tertiary degrees and resides in St. Kilda, Australia.

*You'll find
other outstanding
sports and fitness resources at*

www.HumanKinetics.com

In the U.S. call

1-800-747-4457

Australia.. 08 8277 1555
Canada 1-800-465-7301
Europe...+44 (0) 113 255 5665
New Zealand...................................... 0064 9 448 1207